REWRITING
YOUR HAPPILY EVER AFTER

A Midlife Divorce Survival Guide for Modern Women

Diane Adkins

MINDSTIR MEDIA

Rewriting Your Happily Ever After
Copyright © 2012 by Diane Adkins. All rights reserved.

No part of this book may be used or reproduced in any manner whatsoever without written permission, except in the case of brief quotations embodied in critical articles and reviews. For more information, e-mail all inquiries to: info@mindstirmedia.com

Published by Mindstir Media
PO Box 1681 I Hampton, New Hampshire 03843 I USA
1.800.767.0531 I www.mindstirmedia.com

Printed in the United States of America

ISBN-13: 978-0-9853650-8-0

Library of Congress Control Number: 2012937249

Visit Diane on the World Wide Web:
www.betterbeyonddivorce.com

Author photograph by Revolution Studios, Cary NC

This book is dedicated to all women who have experienced a divorce.

I would like to acknowledge and thank my daughter, Mary Adkins, and my Mother, Mary Mitchell, for believing in me always. I love you! You inspire me every day.

A special note of thanks goes to Don Farrar, my editor, for helping me to make this the best book possible.

I would also like to thank my friends that supported me throughout the many changes in my life over the last several years, and for always encouraging me. A special note of thanks goes to Marquita Thompson, my Life Coach and my friend.

And, I would also like to give a nod to my X − for without him, this book would never have been written.

~ Diane

TABLE OF CONTENTS

PREFACE

"Till death do us part."

Well, it didn't really last that long, did it? As you discovered, living 'happily ever after' doesn't always happen in real life, and for whatever reason your long-term marriage ended.

"How am I supposed to start over at this age?" you may be asking yourself.

If you are anything like me, "Holy *&$! I can't believe this is happening to me! Now what?!!" may have also crossed your mind.

While divorce is devastating at any age, it is often more difficult for women in their 40's and 50's. Middle-aged women often emerge from decades of marriage unsure of how to move forward in their lives.

This book was written for all women who are experiencing or have experienced a divorce at midlife. Regardless of the reasons for the divorce, or who filed, if you are reading this, you're probably looking for some answers about why midlife divorce happens.

More importantly, you want effective techniques to move past the divorce so you can start living as an optimistic, independent woman who is enthusiastic about her future.

Defining yourself as a wife for a long period of time does make it harder to adjust to being a single woman again. *All* those years of marriage have been washed down the proverbial drain. If he walked out on you, it also feels like a major slap in the face.

Make no mistake: Divorce, regardless of the situation, is excruciatingly painful. You are never prepared to deal with the stress, trauma, upheaval and changes caused by the end of a marriage, particularly a long-term one. But believe this: Many women, including me, have suffered the same fate and not only survived, but thrived.

If you are interested in moving past your divorce, carving out your future based solely upon *your* life's purpose, then this is the book for you.

Note that this is not a legal divorce manual. It does not have strategies on how to fix your marriage. It is a divorce recovery guide. The information is geared toward middle-aged women, with the assumption that your children are, at a minimum, in their late teens. But even if your children are young, most of the information will still be useful.

The book is broken down into two parts. This was done so that you have a better understanding of midlife divorce, as well as information and strategies to use as you move past your midlife divorce. I know these strategies are effective because *I* use them, and I'm living proof that you too can, and *will,* survive your midlife divorce.

Part I discusses midlife divorce, midlife crisis and why some men do what they do.

Part II covers the divorce recovery process and provides information, strategies and solutions.

You will also find the following icon **!!** throughout to highlight main points.

For example:
!! *This book addresses midlife divorce and divorce recovery.*

In addition, there are examples of other women's midlife divorce journeys. Their experiences will demonstrate that you too can have a 'happily ever after.'

About now you may be asking yourself, "Why should I listen to you?"

Good question. Here's my short answer: I have lived through and survived my own painful midlife divorce.

Now for the longer answer ...

I married young: 21. My X and I met in college. We fell head over heels in love. We seemed perfect for each other. We liked to do the same things, liked the same movies, had the same sense of humor, and both loved to read. And the clincher: We were *extremely* attracted to each other. I realize that at 21, sex is always red-hot and constant, but back then, I was convinced we were soul mates.

Clearly we had chemistry, and more importantly, we were in love. It was the late eighties ... we were young, broke, in love and just married.

Fast forward 20+ years. Now we're not so young, not broke and married for more than two decades.

Of course, over the years we both had changed, as people do, and our relationship had also morphed — going from a young married couple struggling to pay the bills, to a youngish career couple raising a daughter, to a successful middle-aged couple dealing with not only our own lives, but life in general.

We were *really* busy. We both worked full-time and he traveled a lot for work. In addition, we had the responsibility of our home, raising our daughter, caring for an elderly parent, a dog, and two cats.

Our relationship had become routine, and we were spending less and less time together. Like most married couples, we had our good days and our not-so-good days. We still said "I love you" daily and it appeared — at least to me — that we were both invested in our family and our future.

Was our marriage in the best shape it could have been in? No. Did I ignore some of the signs of trouble? Yes. But I assumed we were in it for the long haul and we would get back to being a 'real couple' after the nest was empty and our lives slowed down.

I trusted that the strong foundation of the life we had built through ups and downs, illnesses, job losses, moves, career changes, car accidents, house sales, births, deaths, and just daily life would always keep the relationship standing. I loved him, and I believed he loved me.

That was, until that fateful Sunday afternoon when he stepped back and aimed a wrecking ball squarely at our marital foundation. It took a direct hit, permanently shattering it.

He was getting ready to leave for a consulting job in Philadelphia. He had finished his shower and he turned to me and flatly announced that he wouldn't be coming home as planned at the end of the week. In fact, he was *never* coming home

He went on to say that he hadn't been happy in twenty years, there was nothing to discuss, and that he wanted out.

Kaboom! The hopes and dreams of 20+ years of marriage were obliterated with a few sentences.

Everything became surreal. I'm not even sure what I said, if anything. It all happened so fast. All I remember is sitting down on the bed because I thought I was going to faint.

He quickly dressed, proceeded to pick up his suitcase — the one I had just finished packing for his business trip — looked over at me crying on the bed, and silently walked out of our bedroom.

He walked downstairs, casually kissed his daughter goodbye, and off he went.

It was at that moment that I really understood what having a nervous breakdown actually feels like. I couldn't control my body. I began twitching, unable to catch my breath. My mind kept replaying the less-than-five-minute encounter I had just had with the man I had spent the last 25 years with — the one who coldly and matter-of-factly announced he was done, finished with his old life, never wanting to be seen nor heard from again.

I was already uneasy. Throughout the past year, we had talked about how burned out I was from my job. I wanted to make a career change. Enter a field more meaningful to me. Something my X had done a few years before. It would mean I'd have to leave a high-paying, secure corporate job that I had held for 14 years to pursue that new career. He pointed out that he was making more than enough money to support the family, and if I really wanted to leave my job, I could and should. So I did.

Within a two-week period, I had left my long-term, high-paying job, and my 23-year marriage came tumbling down. I was 44, unemployed, about-to-be single, and freaking out.

Not only did I have to deal with my marriage being over, I also had to instantly take on all of the responsibilities of the life we spent 20+ years building. All the finances, the house, our daughter who was in her final year of high school, my 83-year-old mother who lived with us, the pets, the cars, and any problem, large or small, that fell under the umbrella of normal adult responsibilities.

After a couple of weeks of wondering what really happened to my marriage, feeling sorry for myself, and generally being miserable, I knew I had my first big decision to make. I could invest a lot of time, money and emotion in finding out what *did* happen, or ... get on with my life.

Even if I could get every answer to each of my questions about my marriage, it would not change one simple fact: My marriage was over. I needed to make my own way in the world, and delving into *my* past was the wrong way to do that.

I needed to find out how other women in similar situations handled things. Not just any women, but the ones who had clawed their way out of their despair and made a *successful* life for themselves and their families. And who now enjoyed their independence, and their success.

In order to do that, I needed to do a lot of research. I buried myself in that research. It was therapeutic.

In addition, it gave me the strength I needed when, believe it or not, he called several months after our separation agreement was signed and asked to come home. As if nothing had happened.

It was clear to me that although I would always care about him, I could no longer be married to him.

We never spoke to each other again.

This new-found information also gave me the emotional strength to help my daughter. My X was also her father and had been very close to her. He now chose to walk away from her, too.

If I would have allowed the focus of that particular part of my life to be only about *him* and not *me* there is a good chance that this book would have been titled "A Midlife Murder — The story of a betrayed wife who took matters into her own hands." or maybe, "The Beginning of the End — A story of how one woman's midlife divorce ruined her life and that of her daughter."

As the months went by, and as I was working through the pain, working with my life coach and reading everything I could get my hands on, I had an epiphany. It was an obvious conclusion that helped awaken me from my emotional stupor, and should help you do so, too:

YOU'RE DIVORCED, NOT DEAD.

The end of your marriage is not the end of your existence nor does it represent a dead end for you. It is just the beginning!

BEGIN YOUR REWRITE

Everyone enters marriage with the idea that it's going to last forever. And yet divorce has become so rampant, hardly anyone is surprised when it happens.

It's left far too many middle-aged women facing divorce.

If it's your husband's infidelity that has ended your marriage, the trauma is magnified. You're left shattered and devastated by the very person who had been the focus of your life, who had become a part of you.

As soon as the word 'divorce' is uttered and the process begins — one of you moves out, lawyers are called, family and friends are told — you come to the frightening realization that you must stand on your own.

Life as you know it may appear to be over.

It's not, but it's about to change.

You may even wonder if there *can* be life for you after the divorce.

Not only *can* there be, there is. And help is on its way.

• • •

FROM BITTER TO BETTER

To start the transition from married to single — and from being bitter to better — you need to first believe everything is going to be all right.

YOU ARE GOING TO BE ALL RIGHT.

It won't be easy. Most days you'll be just fine. But there will be that occasional day when you will not want to face the world.

The information in this book will help you move past those days, and make you look forward to the next day. And the day after that. It's designed to help you change your life for the better. Yes, it's easier said than done. But the important thing is, *it can be done.*

Whether you are facing the first few days of the divorce or you're already picking up the pieces and moving on, this will become your guide as you face your divorce, rebuild your life, handle the many challenges that come with change, and rise above the situation.

Although it may not seem so right now, despite the trauma of divorce, you will not only survive, but move forward, fall in love again — or not — and live 'happily ever after.'

• • •

CHOOSE TO CREATE A NEW STORY

In order to move forward with your life, you need to first move past the 'story' of what you thought your life would be. Stop trying to get back *with* or *at* your X. Get on with your life. To do this you need to start rewriting your 'happily ever after' *today*, under your own terms.

You may need to learn how to be independent, as well as a single parent. You may need to find a new home or apartment, make new friends, or pursue a new career. You may need to sort out your anger and bitterness due to an unwanted divorce. It may also mean you need to face the idea of living without your X who had become your symbol of security for so long.

There are two main components you need in order to rewrite your 'happily ever after' — action and belief.

Take Action
You have to *want* to take action.

That being said, there will be an occasional day when you'll want to pull the blanket over your head. Learn not to cave in. Force yourself out of bed. When you're feeling overwhelmed, you need to concentrate on putting one foot in front of the other.

As the Chinese proverb says, "Talk doesn't cook rice!"

Any type of movement you make is a step in the right direction.

Get up, get going, and get on with your life.

<u>Believe</u>

There can be no true healing without the belief that it is possible. Summon that inner conviction that you have the ability to weather any storm. It is your greatest tool to rise above any adversity, including your midlife divorce.

This will require you to learn how to be more patient and loving with yourself. You will need to learn to push away all the negative thoughts and stop putting yourself down. You will need to work on untying the knot and getting rid of any leftover and lingering attachments you may have to your X.

Perhaps you like it stated a tad more bluntly: If you don't *believe* you can get better, you can't. You can't convince yourself with some little mind trick. The belief has to be front-and-center and without qualification. No ifs, ands or buts. With some items, you can occasionally backslide. Not this one. Sounds almost like a religious belief? Maybe so. But it has to be that strong or you cannot get better. OK, enough tough-guy talk.

You have the power to write your own 'happily ever after.' Be who you want to be and live the life that you truly desire. Own it!

PART I

UNDERSTANDING MIDLIFE DIVORCE

CHAPTER I:
MAKING SENSE OF MIDLIFE DIVORCE

"Sometimes, life not only offers you a fork in the road, but also a spoon and a knife to choose from."

These days more and more marriages start with "I do" and end up with a bitter "I don't anymore."

This chapter will take a look at the increase in midlife divorces, and the reasons why midlife divorce is on the rise. You'll get a brief overview of the impact midlife divorce has on your emotions, your finances and your older/adult children. Having this information will give you a better understanding of midlife divorce before we dive deeper into divorce recovery later on.

• • •

Divorce is more prevalent than ever for those who have been married for decades. There has been a steady increase in midlife divorces over the past years, and it has even been given a name: Grey divorce.

Grey divorce is the term that refers to the increasing trend of divorces for older 'grey-haired' couples that had long-lasting marriages.

Whether you have grey hair or not or whether you initiated your divorce or your X did, it is important to first take a look at the statistical data, so you understand you aren't alone even if it sometimes feels as though you are the only one getting a divorce at midlife.

A CLOSER LOOK AT MIDLIFE DIVORCE STATISTICS

Statistics from the National Center for Family & Marriage Research at Bowling Green State University show that even though the overall divorce rate in the United States has been dropping over the last 20 years, the divorce rate for middle-aged people has doubled. The US Census Bureau reports that the number of divorces in older age groups has increased steadily since 1996.

This increase in midlife divorces is also being felt in other countries as well. In Canada between 1993 and 2003 divorces in the 50 to 54 year old age group rose to 34% and couples between 55 and 59 years old was as high as 48%. The UK divorce statistics also reflect the same trend. In Japan the divorce rate in 2004 was double what it was in 1985 for couples married over 20 years.

You may be wondering why this is happening?

Below are possible causes for the increase in midlife divorces:

• People are living longer.

When men and women hit middle-age they realize that they have a good chance of still having another 40 or so years with their spouse. This sometimes will prompt them to consider taking a second chance. Be it alone or with someone new.

• Over the years, there has been an increase in attention to personal happiness.

This means that men and women are more willing to bail out of an unfulfilling marriage, no matter how long they have been together.

• Women have become less financially dependent on their husband.

Today, more women have successful careers and work outside the home.

Middle-age is also the time of life when financial security is at its strongest.

• The stigma once associated with divorce no longer exists.

• The children are adults or soon will be.
This leads some men and women, who have been staying together for the sake of their children, to go their separate ways.

• The empty nest highlights all the marital problems that were pushed to the background while raising the kids.
Although studies show that many marriages actually improve when the nest empties, an equal number of marriages dissolve.

Some couples look at each other and realize they are virtual strangers, have nothing in common, and are not willing to spend 20, 30 or more years with this stranger.

• Midlife brings with it an emotional roller coaster for both men and women.
Otherwise known as the "midlife crisis."

• Lifestyle and values may have changed over the years, sometimes bringing drug and/or alcohol abuse.

• • •

You may have thought that the longer you are married, the less likely you are to get a divorce; however, it appears that the length of the marriage does not guarantee immunity from divorce. According to some experts, the divorce statistics may trend even higher for late midlife divorces.

It's common when older couples retire, the retirement will contribute to changes in the relationship. The more time spent together could mean more friction and disagreements. Add to that the potential lack of financial freedom and boredom, and these types of changes may strain even 40-year plus marriages to the point of divorce.

!!Statistical data show that midlife divorce, also known as grey divorce, is on the rise.

THE IMPACT OF MIDLIFE DIVORCE

Impact on Emotions

Divorce is hard, and midlife divorce is particularly hard for women. It is an emotional time. We are facing middle age, empty nests, body changes, menopause, and even pending retirement. It is a lot to deal with.

Divorce is a major loss. It is not only the loss of the marriage, it is the loss of a future not realized.

Of course, once a long-term marriage ends, it would be impossible not to feel hurt, betrayal and confusion. Yet it is important to take steps to move past your divorce.

Emotions will come in waves during your recovery process. It is normal for your emotions to go up and down, and for you to feel like you are taking one step forward and two steps back. The important thing to remember is that you have already taken a step in the right direction by educating yourself on midlife divorce and divorce recovery. It takes courage to face a midlife divorce head on.

Midlife divorce will force you to accept that you can't change some things in life, but it will also teach you to become more powerful in changing the things that you *do* have control over.

Sharon was 52 when she came home from work one Monday, asked her husband how his day was and then asked him what he wanted for dinner. Instead of steak or chicken she got a response that would start her on an emotional roller-coaster for the next several years. He didn't want dinner, he wanted a divorce.

Sharon and Robert had recently celebrated their 21st wedding anniversary. They had no children living at home, and just a few weeks earlier they put a large deposit on land up in the mountains. Robert couldn't stop talking about the mountain cabin that they were going to build and how they would move into it permanently when they retired. Because Robert talked and acted as though they would be spending their lives together,

Sharon was caught completely off guard when Robert packed his bags and moved out that Monday night.

It was only a month after Robert officially filed for divorce that Sharon discovered that he had moved immediately from their home into an apartment with a woman 18 years his junior.

Over the following months Sharon's emotional state was shaky at best. She had lost over 20 pounds, couldn't sleep and she knew her constant crying was trying the patience of even her best friends.

The problem was Sharon was emotionally stuck. Even though she knew Robert was living with another woman, and had filed for divorce, she could not accept the fact that the future she had envisioned with Robert was not going to happen. She would spend her nights thinking about that cabin and how she and Robert would grow old together, fishing, boating and relaxing on the lake.

Almost 11 months after that fateful Monday when the final divorce decree came to Sharon's door she finally realized after seeing it in black and white that she needed some help in accepting her new reality.

Sharon spent the next six months working with a professional to accept that her future would include neither Robert nor their cabin. It was then that she started to stop obsessing over a fantasy future that was not going to happen, and grieved the loss of her marriage. She found some self-help tools and strategies that worked for her and started creating and planning her new future.

It has been over four years, and Sharon is now happily remarried, and runs a small scented candle company with her husband. Instead of grieving for a future unrealized, Sharon created her own future.

Impact on Older Children

When dealing with midlife divorce, there is a good chance that your children, if you have any, are in their late teens or are adults. Unlike telling young children who would only need to know a simplified explanation of your divorce and why their Daddy is no longer sharing their house, telling and dealing with an older child may actually prove as difficult, if not more so.

As we learned earlier, a lot of couples put off divorce for the sake of their children. It's a common notion that when the kids are older and on their own or at college the impact of divorce is significantly reduced. It is important to remember that is not necessarily the case.

There are a number of variables that affect the impact that the divorce of their parents has on a child and this does not only include the child's age.

Don't be fooled into thinking that your older or adult children are mature and can just 'handle it.' A parent's divorce can be extremely difficult on children, regardless of their age; if they are living outside the home, and even if they have their own families.

Due to the common notion that older kids will cope better, parents often tend to overlook their children's feelings when dealing with this major family crisis.

A lot of parents often make the mistake of assuming since their children are older or even adults, they will have an easier time coping with the divorce. The reality is that the news of a parent's divorce even to a 25-year-old man can easily turn his world upside down.

It can feel like the rug has been pulled right from under their feet and send their whole world crashing down around them. So, even though you may no longer need to contend with child custody issues, never assume it is going to be easier for your children to take just because they are older.

According to one 30 year old, "If you're an adult when your parents get divorced, you're expected to be able to handle it and just accept it. People don't understand why it's affecting you so hard, but I actually think it can be more detrimental than when you're a child. You find your parents disclosing to you more information than you want to know, and depending on you for support in a way that they wouldn't have when you were a child. Add to that the guilt — both my parents told me that they only stayed together all those years because of me. It's tough, and then you start to question all your childhood memories."

Older children understand divorce, the causes and the impacts far better than a younger child. Because of this, it is critical that you don't feel the need to say too much. Don't provide unnecessary details. While your children are entitled to some form of explanation, the specific details are best left out. Your children are entitled to some protection from a litany of your X's faults, not to mention yours. This will prevent them from feeling pulled or compelled to take sides.

Below are some of the most common issues you should keep in mind regarding your adult children:

• **Remember that your X is also their father.**
Make sure you spare your children from the gory details of your X's sex life, finances, any legal arguments, as well as sharing the emotional angst your X is causing you.

• **Do not expect your children to be your best friend, your surrogate spouse/confidant therapist or life coach.**

• **Never complain about how much time your children spend with your X.**

• **Never tell your children that you only stayed married because of them.**

• **Do not expect your children to hate your X.**

• **Do not expect your children to have the same recovery timeline as yours.**

• **Do not expect your children to be unaffected by the divorce, no matter how old they are.**

• Divorce impacts the family in so many ways, including holidays, vacations, inheritance as well as care giving responsibilities.

Be mindful that these are additional stressors that are being felt by not only you, but also your children.

• Do not expect your children to view the divorce as you do.
To you, you are divorcing your spouse; for your children, it means their parents are divorcing — this comes with a different set of experiences and different point of views.

• Do not expect your children to be happy with the prospect of a new relationship.
Yours or your X's.

• Your children might even be *relieved* to hear that you have filed for divorce.
Children are more perceptive than you think.

!! *A lot of parents often make the mistake of assuming since their children are older or even adults, they will have an easier time coping with the divorce.*

Impact on Finances
In addition to the impact on emotions and your children, in most situations there will be a direct impact on your finances after a midlife divorce.

At midlife you have accumulated assets that younger couples most likely have not, and there are also your retirement funds, joint investments, and insurance to consider. It is at this time that you will find out the hard way what divorce really means from a financial standpoint, and it usually means your financial stability and budget will take a direct hit.

Women almost always tend to experience more significant economic impact following a divorce. The guidelines on equitable

REWRITING YOUR HAPPILY EVER AFTER

distribution are also not helpful for women, especially those with no earned income. Given all these concerns, it is inevitable for you to have some realistic concerns about your economic future as well as your ability to take good care of yourself as you age.

Being diligent and prepared is the key. Do not stick your head in the sand hoping for the best. Also, do not assume that your X will do the right thing and keep your best interests in mind. Divorce brings out the worst in couples, and your situation is most likely no exception. You may want to consider getting a financial advisor. This is the time to be smart about not only your short term financial needs, but also your long term needs.

Below are some of the financial considerations that need to be addressed during a midlife divorce:

• **Pensions**

• **Social Security**

• **Life Insurance**
Did you know that you can still carry life insurance on your X even if you two are divorced?

This is especially important if you are receiving alimony or child support from the X. You want to make sure that you have life insurance on him to cover at least the period of time he is to make payments, so you don't leave yourself open for additional financial problems in case of his death.

Insurance policies have a lot of intricacies when it comes to this. To avoid costly complications, work with an insurance agent.

• **Health Insurance**
You will need to think about medical insurance if you are living in the United States or another country that does not have socialized medicine. The rules differ, so it is critical to find out how the divorce will impact your health insurance coverage and that of any children that are still in school, including college.

Make this one of your top priorities. You do not want to have some health issue come up and find out that you or your children no longer have coverage.

• **Re-Writing of Wills**

• **Tax Exemptions**

• **Insurance Beneficiaries**
You will also need to change the beneficiary on your own life insurance policy. To get your spouse off of your policy you will want to talk to an agent right away.

• **Ownership and Division of Properties**
Resist the urge to fight for things you don't really want to keep; however, if you do want a particular item stand firm.

Do not let the whole process overwhelm you and do not let your X intimidate you into decisions that are not in your best interest. Be firm, but fair.

At this stage in your life you have most likely accumulated a lot, and this is why you must, with absolute certainty, employ a lawyer or a mediator to negotiate your settlement.

Regarding the home: Do **NOT** just automatically state that you want it. **After thorough consideration of the following, you may not want the home:**

• **Be certain that you can take on the mortgage payments.**
You must make sure that you have thought about your income in terms of being single. You will have to decide if this is a payment that you can afford each month.

• **Remember that owing a house includes many more costs than just the monthly mortgage payment.**
Do you feel confident you can afford the ongoing upkeep of the home including emergencies such as a leaking roof?

• Don't make it a contest.

You will also want to think about the fact if you really do want the house and is this really where you want to stay or are you motivated to get the house so that you can claim yourself the 'winner of the house' just to spite your X?

• Is this a good place to make a fresh start?

It is important to really take the time to work through these feelings and then determine if the marital home is really where you want to stay and rebuild your life.

<u>Note</u>: If you are unsure about keeping the house, and you **<u>can</u>** afford to keep it, then it is recommended you negotiate to keep the house. You can always choose to make a change after the divorce is final and you have had more time to work out where you really want to start your new life.

• Children's College Costs

If you have children that are still in college or will be going to college in the near future it is important to remember to address this cost during the divorce negotiations. In the United States, most states do not recognize the need for child support payments after the age of 18. For anyone who has a child in college, they will recognize this law as absurd. Children, particularly adult children, are costly.

!! Be diligent and aware regarding pensions, social security, life and health insurance, home ownership and college costs. This will help to insure you have a solid, workable economic future.

• • •

Now that we have examined some of the statistics regarding midlife divorce and taken a brief look at the impact midlife divorce can have on your emotions, your children and your finances, it is time to get into the heart of the reason for most midlife divorces, the midlife crisis.

CHAPTER II:
THE MIDLIFE CRISIS

"If it wasn't such a cliché, I'd say I'm having a midlife crisis."

If you take into account the growing number of midlife divorces and the men and woman who are claiming their spouses seem to have changed overnight, you know that a midlife crisis is nothing to be blasé about. If you are one of these women who watched their husbands change before their very eyes, you know a midlife crisis when you see it.

In this chapter you will learn more about the triggers of a midlife crisis, internal and external factors that may contribute to the crisis, and what personality types are most likely to have trouble navigating through their midlife years.

Between 40 and 60 most of us will experience some form of a midlife crisis. This phase was first identified by the psychologist Carl Jung, noting that we are totally unprepared for the second half of our life.

This uncertainty on how to move into the next phase causes certain people to carefully take stock of where they are exactly in life and what the adjustments are that need to be made in the way they want to live their lives. What worked during their first 40 or 50 years might not make sense anymore.

It is important to note that most people come through this process smoothly, without making any major life changes. However, if you are reading this, you know that for some a midlife crisis can cause complications that lead to depression, erratic behavior and drastic life-altering decisions.

The term 'midlife crisis' is often used to explain why some individuals choose to do or act a certain way even though they know it can potentially damage or destroy their marriage. The term is widely used, even if certain people are actually years away from midlife.

A midlife crisis is not a medical condition with specific symptoms, a real diagnosis or cure. It can be a short 'blip,' or a 'black hole' leading to the disintegration of a family.

TRIGGERS OF A MIDLIFE CRISIS

So what exactly triggers a midlife crisis? Does it come with the first signs of wrinkles? Is it finding out that exercise does not keep the fat away like it used to? Is it dealing with the fact that you are old and acting young may just help stop the clock? Maybe it is when you realize that the adults you see in those photographs are actually your children.

A few of the signs someone is headed for or in the midst of a midlife crisis include:

• **Physically or mentally leaving your family because you feel trapped and tied down by adult responsibilities.**

• **Doing things that get you into trouble and are out of character.**

• **Hanging out with younger crowds.**

• **Constantly thinking about death.**

• **Trying activities that you stopped doing 20 years ago.**

• **Feeling depressed even when doing tasks that used to make you happy.**

• Wishing you could just run away from everything.

• A new desire to get into physical shape.

• Having bouts of irritability or unexpected anger.

• Desiring risky activities such as skydiving or bungee jumping.

• Buying a lot of new clothes and taking more time to look good.

• Buying an expensive item that wasn't in the budget like a sports car.

In addition to the common activities of people having a midlife crisis they also seem to share the need not to go through this particular passage in life alone. The question then is, is it really necessary to put a marriage at risk in pursuit of midlife happiness?

The answer is, a person in the middle of a midlife crisis doesn't want to be alone, but they don't necessarily want to share this phase of their life with their spouse either. To them it is not about destroying anything, but more on finding the true happiness that they have been seeking.

• • •

There is also internal and external feelings and emotions at work in individuals who go through rough midlife transitions.

Some **INTERNAL** feelings that may be at work during a midlife crisis include:

• Unhappiness with life and their particular lifestyle in general.
This is usually the same lifestyle which provided happiness for the last twenty or more years.

• An inexplicable resentment over their marriage.
Blaming everything from unhappiness with a job to unhappiness with the way they look on fact that they are married. If they weren't

married they would look better, have a better career and basically a better life.

• A strong desire for a new and more passionate relationship.

There is most likely a strong belief that the desire and passion of a new relationship will continue forever.

• Boredom with things and people who have been of interest to them before.

Unfortunately, the number one person identified in this category is usually the spouse.

• Feeling the need for some change and adventure.

There is the idea that there has to be more to life than work, family and a home.

• The questioning of certain life choices and the need to validate the decisions made years ago.

They begin to look at others with envy, specifically at younger people or singles that seem to be living a much more exciting life.

• Uncertainty about who they are and how they are spending their lives.

There is a feeling that if they don't make a change now, it will be too late.

• Doubt if they truly loved their spouse.

Rationalization that since they never truly loved their spouse, they want to find 'true love' before they die.

Some **EXTERNAL** factors that may lead a person to experience a difficult time during midlife include:

• Debt and Responsibility

Facing ongoing debt or an increase in debt from sources such as their children's college tuition, and the nearing possibility of retirement can add more stress to an already demanding and stressful life.

While it would be more logical to seek assistance from a debt management company or work with your spouse on a budget, people who are experiencing a midlife crisis often find it easier to simply walk away from their families just to escape from what they perceive is the cause of their debt.

• Significant Loss and Facing Mortality

A death of a loved one will naturally cause grief, which can be difficult to accept and come to terms with. For people going through a difficult midlife transition, a loss can be more overwhelming for them.

By midlife, most of us have experienced death — whether it is the death of a parent or someone else close to us or the death of a co-worker or friend. It can be even be more devastating if the person who died is near to your age.

Experiencing loss is a strong reminder to many that life is short and we are mortal; however, for those in the midst of a crisis — an event like this can add fuel to the fire in justifying out of character actions and decisions.

• Avoidant and Anxious Personality

Some people who have the natural tendency to avoid conflict in their relationships will often find it difficult to navigate smoothly through midlife. In addition to low self-esteem and the need for acceptance, this type of personality often has feelings of inadequacy and an extreme sensitivity to negative evaluation which usually keeps them from reaching out and seeking help. They will find it easier to run away from their problems instead of finding possible solutions. These personalities commonly end up in divorce court during midlife.

Clearly there are both internal and external factors that can aggravate the midlife transition process. For many people who lack understanding of what they are going through or are unable or unwilling to get professional help will often find themselves making irrational decisions which they may later regret, such as divorcing their spouse, leaving a job, or throwing away the security that they have built over the years.

Theresa and Bill had been married for almost 28 years. They had been high school sweethearts, and married two years after graduation. They had raised two daughters and a son, and just had their first grandchild when one of their best friends from high school died suddenly of a massive heart attack at the age of 47.

Neither of them could believe that their friend had died, and so young. He was their age!

Both had been affected by the loss of their friend, but Bill who had always had trouble sharing his feelings began to change almost overnight. He had always been easy going, and recently had started to argue with Theresa on every little thing. He also started to hang out at the local bar — something he had stopped doing in his early twenties after their first daughter was born.

Bill's personality changes, along with his late nights at the bar were starting to take a toll on their marriage. Theresa knew that her husband was going through some sort of crisis, and that it was probably brought on by the death of their high school friend. She was trying to be patient, but his actions were affecting her emotional and physical health.

Over a six month period of the 'new Bill', Theresa tried to talk to him. She asked him to stop going to the bar, stop drinking and basically stop acting like a teenager. She pointed out that his behavior was dangerous and that he was jeopardizing his marriage and everything they had both worked so hard for. Bill wanted to hear none of it. In one of their last arguments on the subject, Bill told Theresa he felt trapped and that he was moving out.

Theresa, having spent multiple sleepless nights worrying if her husband had wrapped his car around a pole or was wrapping himself around another woman, didn't try to convince Bill that he should stay.

Three months after he moved out, he called Theresa, and wanted to come home. The first thing Theresa wanted to know was had he stopped going to the bar and was he willing to do marriage counseling and get help for his drinking problem? The answer was no on all counts, and that was also the answer that Theresa gave Bill. It was clear that Bill did not want to take any responsibility for his actions and it was clear he was not willing to give up his nights at the bar even if it meant losing his marriage. It appeared to Theresa that the 'new Bill' was here to stay.

During the months after Bill left, Theresa, in an effort to help herself cope, had begun to work on her own personal development. She had learned and now fully understood that the only person that she could change was herself. She also understood that although she would always love Bill, she could no longer have him in her life. She filed for divorce that week.

!! *A midlife crisis is not a medical condition with a specific set of symptoms, a real diagnosis or cure. It can also be a short 'blip,' or a 'black hole' leading to the disintegration of a family.*

FUNNY IN THE MOVIES, BUT NOT SO MUCH SO IN REAL LIFE

A midlife crisis is far from being a happy-go-lucky phase of an individual's life. This goes for the person having the crisis as well as the spouse and family.

Among the most common behavioral changes of a midlife crisis are the following:

Infidelity
Many people going through a midlife crisis cheat. This may be caused by the need to prove desirability and sexuality or from boredom

or dissatisfaction with their spouse. Quite naturally, infidelity can cause a damaging blow to any marriage and in many cases leads to divorce.

Impulsive Behavior

People who are dealing with a midlife crisis are known to act impulsively, such as quitting their jobs or making some extraordinarily extravagant purchases without consulting their spouse. This often causes serious financial strain within the marriage, which can potentially lead to divorce.

Lack of Communication

Over the years, it is common for some long-term marriages to grow complacent which can result in a general lack of communication. When a spouse goes through some mental and emotional issues associated with a midlife crisis, this communication problem is multiplied, causing the marital relationship to eventually fall apart.

• • •

From experience, you may already know that one of the most impacted areas of life during a midlife crisis is marriage. Even the happiest and longest unions can be sorely tested when individuals are entangled in the deep throes of a midlife crisis.

While the movies portray a midlife crisis by showing women getting boob-lifts and dressing like teenagers and men buying a sports car or a boat, the reality is that the other more risky, abrupt, and sudden decisions people make during a midlife crisis cause real, deep hurt to their spouse and children and can cause themselves deep regret in the long run.

!! *The most common behavioral changes of a midlife crisis include infidelity, impulsive behavior and lack of communication.*

• • •

You now understand the triggers of a midlife crisis, some of the internal and external factors that may contribute to having a midlife crisis, and what personality types are most likely to have trouble navigating through their midlife years. The next chapter will address an area you may have a great interest in learning more about — the *male* midlife crisis.

CHAPTER III:
THE MALE MIDLIFE CRISIS

"Who is that man in the mirror?"

In this chapter we will take an in-depth look at what goes on in the heads of some men at midlife. Please note the word **'some'**, not all. That is a critical distinction because it is very important to recognize that not all men go through the type of crisis described in this chapter.

The purpose of this chapter is to give you, the woman who is going through midlife divorce recovery; some much needed information as to why your X may have acted the way he did.

It cannot be stressed enough that this chapter is not to prove that your X or men in general, are immature, selfish, and self-centered. It is also not to prove how women are mature and unquestionably correct. We all know both statements aren't true.

It is also not to state that all midlife divorces are the result of a **male** midlife crisis. As we have already established, most men and women go through this phase of their lives with little to no trouble, and there are usually a multitude of contributing factors involved when looking at the cause of divorce after a long-term marriage.

The intent of this chapter is to help you gain a better understanding of the crisis some men encounter at midlife, so you can gain a better understanding of the possible reasons your X may have changed into a virtual stranger overnight.

Although understanding why some men do what they do won't necessarily help ease your pain, it should at least educate you on the possible reasons why your X behaved the way he did if indeed a midlife crisis was a prime contributor to your divorce.

So, what does a male midlife crisis look like? Many men going through a midlife crisis often start fantasizing about younger women or have the unexplained desire to purchase a sports car. Some men will go on a crash diet or dream of being free from all their adult responsibilities. They have an increased desire for a 'do-over' of their life.

A reason for this may be that men at midlife usually come face to face with the fact that they really are going to die someday. Maybe a parent has died or a friend or co-worker that was near to their own age. This struggle with mortality can cause a sense of panic and the need to experience, start or finish all the things they wanted to do in their own lives.

These men seem to wake up one day and the hard reality hits them right in their gut: they are not going to live forever. They then start to notice their bodies have really started to age, their waist is bigger and their hair is greying or is completely gone. On top of that, reading glasses become a necessity.

So they have sagging skin, new wrinkles, and to add insult to injury, they may be experiencing a dwindling sex drive which just adds fuel to the midlife crisis fire. Add in those small aches and pains in their joints and you can somewhat understand why some men go to such lengths to desperately cling to their youth by engaging behaviors such as dressing in trendier clothing, taking up exciting activities such as car racing or going after women half their age.

It appears that men caught in a midlife crisis are scared to death of facing the prospect of growing old. As these men come to realize that life is indeed passing by, unfortunately, they also often see their wives as the person who is holding them down and shackling them to a life they no longer wish to participate in.

Some men will also rewrite their history and portray you as a nag, your marriage as dull and draining, and your family life as boring and lacking meaning. Research shows that once a man has started a rewrite there is little to nothing you can say or do that will change his new view on his old life.

Julie and Kevin had been married for 20 years when Julie decided to do a little snooping on her husband's computer when she noticed he hadn't signed out when he went to work. Kevin had been spending an inordinate amount of time on the computer and would shut the screen off the minute she walked in the room. He told her it was just work, but this behavior coupled with the drastic change in his personality and the fact that he was never interested in sex, made her decide to take a look.

Julie uncovered several porno sites that her husband had joined, but that was not the worst thing.

Sitting in her husband's email was what appeared to be very intimate correspondence between her husband and a woman who signed her named "C."

As she read through the back and forth correspondence it became clear that her husband was heavily involved with this woman, at least via the internet, but something else also became clear. Her husband — the man she raised a child with, the one who had always made her laugh, the one she had just returned from a one week vacation to Florida with was not only having a cyber-affair, but had portrayed her as some sort of evil woman. She was described as 'nagging', 'overbearing', and a 'control-freak of a wife' who was as 'cold as ice' in bed. She also learned that somehow the years they spent together raising their son had actually been 'the longest 18 years' of her husband's life, and that he had only 'stayed for the kid'. Now that the kid was in college, he was finally going to be 'free.' The final email she read described their recent vacation as a 'trip to hell' that he couldn't wait to return from.

Julie confronted Kevin only to have him actually repeat everything that the emails had said about their marriage, their life together and her in particular. Julie tried to point out that he was 'rewriting' their history, and was portraying her as someone she wasn't. Kevin told her to "go to hell" and stormed off.

After a few days, Julie approached Kevin again. After calming down, she realized that he must be going through some sort of crisis; she still loved him and was willing to try and save the marriage. Julie suggested marriage counseling and he agreed.

Unfortunately, it became clear after several sessions that Kevin was holding strong to his version of the marriage and of Julie. Julie also found him masturbating in front of his computer, and when she questioned his behavior he told her it was 'none of her damn business.' Kevin never showed for another counseling session. Julie decided she wanted a better life, and that it was time to make a drastic change. Julie has since moved out, and is working on rebuilding her self-esteem, and is waiting for the divorce to be final.

In addition, some men have grown tired of feeling responsible for so long — mortgages, bills, the wife, the kids, tuition, all of which forces them to be stuck going to work week in and week out. This can lead to depression and they believe that the only salvation is to be free from the marriage so they are able to pursue their own personal goals and happiness — without their wives and responsibilities slowing or weighing them down.

It goes without saying that the behavior of the man caught in a real midlife crisis causes an unbelievable amount of pain, hurt and confusion to the man's wife and family, but it appears that the men in crisis either don't see this or don't want to see this. Rationalization seems to run rampant during a male midlife crisis.

THEMES OF A MALE MIDLIFE CRISIS

To help you better understand the male midlife crisis let's explore some of the more prominent themes.

Following are some of the major themes that are common to men who are having a midlife crisis:

Life as a Never-Ending Burden

For many men who are experiencing a midlife crisis they start to resent their role as a provider to their families.

These men see these 'sacrifices' as keeping them from having the life they envisioned. Instead of looking at what they have in their lives, loving and caring relationships, challenging work, friendships, and stability, they view their lives as a burden that they are being forced to endure.

It is important to remember, you and your children are no one's 'burden.' If a man is unable to see this, he is not someone you want or need in your life.

The Unrealized Dream or Fantasy Life

Many men that are in the throes of a midlife crisis still have not let go of the unrealistic ambitions or goals they may have had from an early age. Old dreams die hard, and if a man is not able to appropriately adjust his dreams and goals throughout his life, it may result in constant discouragement and unhappiness.

As you may know, the reality is that your X most likely would not have become the President or the lead singer of a rock band, even if he had not married or had children. During his crisis, he may not.

Unfortunately, men in the middle of a midlife crisis tend to believe that their adolescent dreams of success and fortune would have happened and still may happen if they just can get rid of the shackle, you the wife, which holds him back.

Your X may cling to a set of unrealistic dreams, and because they have not come to fruition it is easy to blame you.

Now, unless you kept him locked in a closet for the last 20 years; you have not kept him from achieving his dreams. This is his issue.

I Want (no, *Need*) a New Life

There are certain men who during a midlife crisis are faced with the overwhelming need to leave their jobs or families and do just that, much to the shock of those around him. This crisis is often brought about by the powerful need for a man to redefine or reinvent himself once he reaches midlife.

He believes that his old life — including you and sometimes even his children, his home, his career and other areas of his everyday life — no longer works for him.

He may also believe you no longer are or never were his true love.

These men believe if they can just get rid of you, that their perfect woman is waiting out there ready to be found or in some cases has already been found. In their minds, this new woman is willing to give them all the attention and none of the nagging, while, of course, looking fit and beautiful.

As you may already know, but a man in the middle of a midlife crisis doesn't, changing the external things in your life without working on the internal issues, will never fix anything. Your X may have walked out on his life assuming that his new and improved life, less you and your children will make everything right with him — unfortunately that is rarely the case. In the meantime, his selfish (and there really isn't another word for it) actions along with his inconsiderate behavior has already caused irreparable damage to you and your children that will most likely never be repaired.

So, how does a man just walk away from his family ... the life he spent decades building? How does he ruin the relationships he has worked years building with his wife and children, without so much as a care?

Only the man who has done this knows the answer to that one.

For many women it most likely will always be somewhat incomprehensible how one can just walk out, walk away and never look back. It is doubtful that these women will ever really comprehend what he was thinking. If this has happened to you, stop searching for answers you may never get, and start concentrating on you and your future and your happiness.

The three scenarios above are examples of what can occur when a man is confronted with a midlife crisis. There most likely are others that haven't been addressed, but the main thing to understand is, as you know, some couples are able to move past a male midlife crisis, while unfortunately, others crash and burn with it.

• • •

Before moving on to further explore the male midlife crisis it is important to look at one other theme — which technically doesn't fall under the male midlife crisis definition, but should be addressed in order to give a well-rounded look at men during their midlife transition.

Re-Evaluation and Reflection

Some men will hit midlife and begin to turn inward and take a hard look at his own life to determine where he is and where he would like to be.

It is at this time, he may discover that he no longer wishes to be married or he no longer is in love with you and he would like to explore the next chapter of his life by himself or with someone new. It would be an unfair generalization to lump this type of rational decision making by a man into the midlife crisis category.

It may be a hard fact to acknowledge, but your X may be one of these men.

!! Upon reaching a certain point in life, men struggle with the reality of mortality, which causes that sense of panic and the need to experience or finish all the things they wanted to do in their own lives.

THE TIME IS RIPE FOR A MALE MIDLIFE CRISIS

It is difficult to pinpoint the exact age when a man will experience his midlife crisis. As we already know, if often strikes men in their late-30s to their early-50s. Some men confess that while they love their wives, they are no longer *in love* with them, resulting in unhappiness and discontent.

At this point in a man's life he usually can also afford to have a midlife crisis. In this world, there are two types of currency, money and time — both of which can serve as fuel for men to tiptoe toward a full blown midlife crisis. Having both time and money can lead to opportunities, which ultimately results in temptations such as the new luxury sports car or in many cases it is in the form of a new woman, usually younger.

!! *Middle-age is a point in a man's life where he usually can afford to have a midlife crisis.*

SO, WHY DO SOME MEN AT MIDLIFE CHEAT?

Before examining why some men cheat at midlife, it is important in this internet age to define cheating. No one would argue that having sex with someone other than your spouse is cheating. What about having long, intimate conversations via email or in a chat room? How about viewing pornography or going to a strip club?

Books could be written on this topic, and most likely already have, but for this purpose cheating is defined as one or more of the following:

• Having sexual relations outside of your marriage.

• Participating in activities or relationships that you know full well your spouse would have good reason to be angry and/or upset about.

• Participating in activities or relationships where you need to make up excuses to justify your actions or where you feel the need to lie to your spouse.

Of course, your personal definition of cheating may be broader or much narrower. The bottom line is that if you have cheated or have been cheated on, the act can devastate your spouse and be the death blow of even long-term marriages.

So why do some men cheat at midlife?

All the aforementioned factors often experienced by men having a midlife crisis can contribute to the need to cheat.

As we learned earlier, a man may have convinced himself that he is no longer in love with you or that you are the cause of all of his pain and anguish. Because of this he rationalizes that it is acceptable to pursue other women.

It can stem from the feeling of boredom or the need to prove his prowess with younger women and the need for him to maintain virility.

There is also the sad and hard truth that he may have really fallen in love with someone else. This may not be what you want to read, but it is a fact. People sometimes do fall in love with someone other than the one they married.

Of course, you cannot also discount the availability of willing women and the nonstop temptations married men face. Not to mention the way that television and movies portray how virile a man should be. Now, if your X is a serial cheater, then a midlife crisis is definitely a lame excuse for cheating on you, yet again.

However it comes to be, once your husband cheats, you are left with a self-esteem that has been shattered, your relationship no longer seems real, and the rug of your secure marriage has been ripped right from under your feet.

Beth and Jonathon had just driven their son to college, and both talked on the way home about how nice it would be to finally have an empty house. They of course would miss their son, but it would be nice to spend more time together as a couple, going out to dinners, and having some fun. They had always had a fulfilling sex life, and Beth imagined it would most likely even get better now that they didn't have to worry about a teenager in the house.

It was a second marriage for both of them, but by this point they had been married over 16 years, and Jonathon had officially adopted her son from her first marriage.

The trouble began only a few weeks into their empty nest. Beth noticed that Jonathon was working a lot more than usual. Jonathon assured Beth that he would love to be coming home on time, but he was under a deadline at work. Jonathon was a Technology Director at a large IT company, and this wasn't the first time that he had a deadline, so Beth had no reason not to believe him. That was until she opened the American Express bill.

The balance was almost twenty-five thousand dollars and the October bill alone was close to eight thousand dollars. Most of the charges were for a place called The White Room.

There were over twenty charges in October varying from two hundred to over five hundred each, so Beth assumed their card number had been stolen and that this was a mistake. She quickly called the card company. They assured her that the charges were legitimate and that they were all signed for by Jonathon. Beth realized that arguing the point with this particular customer service representative was of no use, so she looked up the address of The White Room, and took a ride.

Beth sat in the parking lot, trying to make sense of everything. The White Room was actually a gentlemen's club — a classier version of a strip joint.

At this point, Beth was still under the assumption that their card had been stolen, so she got out of her car and walked right into the place. Beth had never been inside a gentlemen's club, and was shocked to see that it was not trashy at all, but very high class. It looked like a fancy restaurant. That is if fancy restaurants now came with half naked woman dancing on the table or women straddling and grinding into their customers as they sat back in their chairs. It even had a gift shop of sorts that sold outfits for the girls, as well as adult accessories.

It was in there that she spotted her husband. He was in the middle of purchasing some slinky bright pink lingerie for the very young, half naked woman who was hanging from his arm.

Beth later found out the girl's name was Jennifer and not 'gold digger' as Beth often referred to her. She was all of 22, an exotic dancer, and the woman who Jonathon not only was spending a lot of money on, but who he had decided he was meant to be with.

Beth ultimately filed for divorce, and is now working on rebuilding her life. It has been hard on both Beth and her son, but Jonathon seemed to make the transition completely out of both of their lives with what appeared to be little to no trouble. Beth is now working on grieving the loss of her marriage and more importantly the loss of the man she thought she was married to for all those years.

From the statistical evidence, there are many women hurt, shattered, and betrayed. Studies show that approximately 40% of men seek sexual satisfaction outside their relationships.

The facts are that just because a lot of men are cheating, it does not give a man carte blanche to do the same. Midlife is also not a valid excuse.

There are marriages that survive infidelity; however, if you are reading this, your marriage was not one of them. You are on the right path in trying to get a firm understanding of why men cheat, especially during midlife. This will enable you to better understand that your X needs to take responsibility for his actions, and it is your responsibility to start taking care of you!

!! *Infidelity leads to hurt, betrayal and shattered lives.*

WHY MARRIED MEN LEAVE FOR YOUNGER WOMEN

Why do middle-aged men prefer to date 20-somethings and even put their happy marriage and successful life at serious risk just to pursue these women?

There are a number of reasons why older men in their 40's and 50's cave in to the temptation of having an affair with women almost half their age.

Young = Exciting and Ego Boost
Young = Slim, Trim, Flawless Bodies
Young = Carefree Lives; No Responsibilities

In addition, in long-term marriages you will eventually start to complement each other less and gradually grow to take each other for granted. Over the years women often are no longer able to give their undivided attention to their husband — understandably so with so many demands of juggling family life and career.

This emotional disconnection between a wife and husband who have been together for a good number of years gives both the feeling of being under-appreciated. According to some men, it is the lack of kind gestures and thoughtfulness that drive them to cheat.

Men, in general, like to be appreciated. Because men also often have a skill of finding women who are easily impressed (young and naïve), and these younger women are willing to step in and fill the gap by showing them appreciation and interest, it can be too much of a temptation to resist.

In addition, a middle-age man has already accumulated many life experiences. What may be boring or common to one woman, you — the wife of many years — can be quite fascinating to another female, the new woman.

It is also important to note that younger women often seek the company of older men. This is because they view older men as having authority, more stability and, of course let us not forget, more financial success then men closer to their own age.

With these types of enticements, it is no wonder that men, especially during a midlife crisis, are tempted — choosing to destroy the trust in their long term marriage, and, in many cases, leading them right into divorce court.

There is also the fact that numerous television ads and movies tell him that either every other husband and wife are enjoying wild, passionate sex in between going to work, food shopping, and taking their kids to college or the man is portrayed as middle-aged, single and having sex with every young girl that he passes on the street.

He questions why shouldn't he have that?

Why? Because it just isn't realistic, it's the movies. However, by now, you know that logic and midlife crisis do not necessarily go together.

It is clear that the stable and simple routine of family life and everything that comes with it including a supportive, loving family is no longer enough for many men, especially once a midlife crisis hits.

So, what exactly do some middle-aged men want these days? Maybe just a little too much.

THE DO'S AND DON'TS OF SURVIVING INFIDELITY AT MIDLIFE

DON'T'S

• Don't beat yourself up.

Your X has already done enough damage for the both of you. Your self-esteem and self-confidence can really take a hit when it comes to infidelity.

It is important to remember that celebrity couples break up all the time due to infidelity, which goes to show that no matter how attractive or successful you are, it does not make you immune to the possibility of your husband cheating on you, especially during a midlife crisis.

• Don't dwell on the details of your husband's infidelity.

Accept the fact that there is nothing you can possibly do to change the past. Going through the whole scenario and dwelling too much on what happened can cause emotional scarring.

Focus your energies on growing beyond the pain instead of obsessing over the very cause of your pain.

• Don't isolate yourself.

During this period, it is all too easy to just hole up, but isolating yourself will only make your pain worse.

Force yourself to go out and explore the new life waiting ahead of you. Your X cheated on you, but don't let him cheat you out of the rest of your life.

DO

• Do work on your personal development.

Work on restoring your self-esteem, building your confidence, and learning something new. Read, study and concentrate on you.

• Do make some changes.

Get a new haircut, buy some new clothes, and change up your environment.

• Do make more time for yourself.

Take more time to pamper yourself. The most reliable person who can accept and love you through this difficult time is you.

• Do get support.

Surround yourself with people who truly have your best interest at heart. This includes a therapist and/or a life coach.

Do NOT give your X the power over your life. You have the ability to weather this storm and move in the direction of a brighter future.

FEMALE MIDLIFE CRISIS: IS THERE SUCH A THING?

It may come as a surprise for many, but women are not totally immune to a midlife crisis.

It is important to note there are some women who have midlife crisis on par with a man's — cheating, dressing too young, leaving their husbands and families high and dry, etc. — but, research shows these women are in the minority. For most women the transition is less a crisis and more a positive, eye-opening experience.

Like men, a women's need for change at midlife is triggered by events in their life such as the death of a parent, a spiritual journey or job loss.

Unlike the male midlife crisis however, the female version tends to be more optimistic and centers on re-evaluating their lives. It tends to be a time for self-reflection and re-prioritization.

What is truly happing during a female midlife crisis is the process of self-rediscovery. Since women spend the first 40 or 50 years of their lives raising their children, taking care of their families, their husbands, their home and their careers, midlife is finally the time they can focus more on their own needs.

As the nest empties, a woman finally has the time to turn inward and take a look at her life to figure out where she is and where she would like to be. It is at this time, that a woman may discover that the job she has always held no longer works for her or her 'status quo' marriage needs work or needs to end. It is no wonder that many midlife divorces are requested by women.

!! The female "midlife crisis" tends to be more optimistic and centers on re-evaluating their lives.

MIDLIFE CRISIS DOES NOT ALWAYS EQUAL MIDLIFE DIVORCE

There are other factors that may come into play with regard to midlife divorce and midlife crisis is just one.

Other factors that contribute to a midlife divorce include:

• **You and your husband have grown irreparably apart.**

• **You fight constantly over every little issue.**

• **You and your husband no longer enjoy spending time together.**

• **You and your husband are no longer are in love.**

Whether the divorce was the result of one of these factors or was the result of a midlife crisis, yours or his, the important thing is it happened. You now need to avoid blaming yourself and your X for what was done, what wasn't done or what you both could have done differently. It is time to focus your attention to moving on from your marriage and your divorce. You need to start pursuing your own personal happiness, as an independent woman.

Moving on from a midlife divorce involves untangling the complex connections that have developed over decades of marriage. However, a lot of women out there are surprised to look back and realize that their divorce actually was a blessing in disguise that opened up a whole new world of opportunities for them. You too can also start writing your own success story, not just merely about surviving divorce, but by building a more rewarding and successful life beyond it — your own version of 'happily ever after'.

So, now that you understand a bit more about midlife divorce and midlife crisis, it is time now to move on to Part II Divorce Recovery — and start creating the life you want to have after your midlife divorce.

PART II

DIVORCE RECOVERY

CHAPTER IV:
YOU ARE NOT YOUR DIVORCE

"Look at divorce not as a death, but as a rebirth of the real you."

A lot of women, faced with the end of their decades-long marriage, feel like they have failed in some way. They allow their midlife divorce to dictate not only their past and present, but also their future. Part II of this book will help to make sure that you are not one of those women.

It is critical to your recovery that you understand and believe that your marriage, and the end of it, does not define you or your future. This chapter will start you on your way by giving you a brief overview of what the divorce recovery process is.

To be clear, there is absolutely nothing wrong with taking time to analyze what contributed to the breakdown of your marriage; however, dwelling too much on the 'why's' is not a productive way to face the challenges ahead of you.

Don't get stuck with the *"what if's"* and the *"should haves."* This repetitive thinking is not good for you, and can be detrimental to your self-esteem and your ability to move through the divorce recovery process. While reflecting on what went wrong will enable you to avoid a repeat of the same type of relationship in the future is recommended, the point here is NOT to dwell on the "If I just would have" or "If he just would have" scenarios.

• • •

WHAT EXACTLY IS DIVORCE RECOVERY?

Divorce recovery is the emotional process of moving through and past your midlife divorce, establishing yourself as a healthy, independent woman with her own purpose.

Every divorce is unique and personal, but it can help to know and understand that the emotional confusion you are experiencing and the sadness, anger, bitterness and every other emotion under the sun will improve over time.

Divorce recovery addresses the 'softer' side of the divorce. The legal and financial side of the divorce is handled by your lawyer, but the emotional side of the divorce needs to also be addressed and worked through — this is the Divorce Recovery Process.

The following are some areas that divorce recovery includes:

• Working through all the emotional stages of divorce.

• Grieving the death of not only your marriage, but of a future not realized.

• Acknowledging and accepting that the divorce is a reality.

• Coping with all the changes.

• Re-examining your life to clarify and set compelling goals.

• Working on your personal development.

!! Don't get stuck with the "what if's" and the "should haves". This repetitive thinking is not good for you and can be detrimental to your self-esteem and your divorce recovery.

HOW LONG DOES 'TYPICAL' DIVORCE RECOVERY TAKE?

There is no set guideline on how fast or slow you will recovery from your midlife divorce. Some experts have said that it takes a full year for every five years you were married to fully move through the process; however, that is very subjective because just like everyone's marriage is unique, your divorce process and recovery will also be unique.

Some additional factors include:

• **Did the divorce come out of the blue or was a long time coming?**

• **The length of your marriage.**

• **How well you and your X got along before the divorce.**

• **Is your X already involved in a new relationship?**

• **Was infidelity involved in the decision to divorce?**

• **Your personality. His personality.**

• **Was the divorce amicable or nasty?**

• **And 100 other possible factors. ...**

Unfortunately, when it comes to getting over the pain of your midlife divorce there is no magic button that can be hit so that you can just skip over going through the divorce recovery process.

However, below are some ways you can help yourself along the divorce recovery road:

• **Allow yourself time to grieve your loss.**

• **Allow yourself to feel and experience whatever emotions you are feeling.**

• **Invest time on your personal development.**

• **Be positive.**

• Accept your situation, and choose to move on when it's appropriate to move on.

If you are finding it impossible to move through the divorce process or it has been an inordinate amount of time since your divorce, say three or four years, you are most likely preventing yourself from fully recovering, and in turn, are missing out on opportunities to improve your life and your future.

No matter what stage you are in, try to embrace the information in this book and also consider professional help — you just may need that little push to get you started down the road to recovery.

Sheila's marriage ended a little over three years ago. She had been married for 22 years to Paul, and when their youngest daughter was in her final year of high school they made the decision, jointly, to get a divorce. Their older daughter was a sophomore at college, and they didn't see the point in putting off the inevitable any longer.

They had tried marriage counseling, and it just seemed that nothing could fix their relationship. They didn't fight, but they also didn't really speak. They loved each other, but more in a brother-sister way than a husband-wife way. They had drifted apart over the years while juggling their careers and raising their children and it appeared to both of them that they were too far apart to ever get back together again. The only common ground they had was their daughters.

The divorce process was amicable. They divided their property fairly, and Paul agreed to give Sheila the house. From the beginning of the divorce process Paul continued to be very involved with and close to both of his daughters, and he still played an active role in their lives. He bought a townhouse five miles away, and both daughters would stay with him occasionally during school breaks and summer vacations.

Paul also stayed in contact with Sheila. Because he only lived a few miles down the road, he would come over to mow the lawn and fix anything around the house that needed to be fixed. Sheila would call him if her car broke down or if she needed something brought down from the attic. In return, Sheila would pick up groceries for Paul occasionally or do some of his laundry. She would even send a home cooked meal home with him from time to time when he stopped by.

From the outside it looked as if it was the 'nicest' divorce that two people could hope to have.

Paul seemed happy with the new arrangement and he had started dating right after the final divorce was issued. He wasn't looking for a serious relationship; he was just enjoying meeting new people. Sheila on the other hand, had not tried dating, even though one of the men at her work had asked her out not once, but three different times. Sheila felt that since she couldn't make her long-term marriage work with Paul, who was clearly such a nice guy, what chance did she have with someone new.

Then one day, one of the ladies Sheila worked with encouraged her to go with her to a divorce seminar that was being held locally. Sheila didn't believe she would get much out of it since she had been divorced going on four years.

Much to Sheila's surprise, she did. She discovered that although she had divorced Paul years ago, she had not learned to actually live without him. She learned that she had failed to really acknowledge that she was no longer married to Paul and that she needed to set boundaries. She depended on Paul too much and she was still acting in some ways as a wife to him. All of this had prevented her from moving on with her own life as an independent woman and kept her from exploring new relationships with other men.

Over the next few weeks, she set some new boundaries. She asked Paul to stop dropping by unannounced. She informed him that she hired someone to cut the grass. She also made a rule that she would no longer called him when something in the house broke or her car wouldn't start.

Sheila finally started to accept her situation, and started to concentrate on learning how to live separately from Paul. She also concluded that Paul was a nice guy, but he was no longer her husband, and it was time to let go and move on.

So, again, how long will this take?

Well, think of your midlife divorce in terms of two spiders that have been spinning a web together for decades. Clearly, the longer the two spiders were together, the more tangled their web will be, and so it will take time to untangle their webs and go on their separate ways. Since these spiders have been together for a long time, in addition to them physically separating, it will also take time to emotionally separate themselves from each other and grieve the loss of their relationship.

!! *When it comes to getting over the pain of your midlife divorce, unfortunately, there is no magic button that can be hit so that you can just skip over going through the divorce recovery process.*

• • •

Now that you have a better understanding of what makes up the divorce recovery process, you can move on to understanding the midlife divorce grieving process and why it is a necessity to grieve the death of your marriage.

CHAPTER V:
THE DEATH OF A MARRIAGE

"The grieving process is like rafting down a river, just when you relax and believe you are on smooth waters you hit the rapids."

Grief is normal after a midlife divorce and it is not unusual to go through long periods of sadness and depression, especially in the beginning. This chapter will help you to understand the need to grieve the loss of your long-term marriage, will help you to identify where you may be in the process and will give you practical ideas to manage your emotions.

During the first few weeks after the decision to divorce is made it takes a while for everything to sink in and for you to start adjusting to life without your X. It can be quite challenging to make any decisions, much less think clearly. It's okay. It will get better with time.

If you are farther down the path of divorce recovery, you most likely remember well those first few weeks and months, and you can attest that time helps.

Dealing with death of a marriage has been compared to the death of a loved-one without the flowers and sympathy cards.

Melanie felt that her family and friends didn't really understand the need for her to grieve the end of her 15 year marriage to Michael. Her marriage had been fraught with upset, almost from the beginning. Melanie had been pregnant when they married, and Michael really never acted as if he wanted to be a father or a husband.

Once the baby arrived, life seemed to take over, and before she knew it five years had passed, then ten and then fifteen. Melanie felt their lives were comfortable, although not exactly happy. Melanie also wanted to avoid causing upset to their teenaged son, so she accepted her relationship and her marriage as is. It was Michael who finally pulled the plug. He had met someone at work and was in love.

Melanie couldn't blame him. Their relationship was basically two people living under the same roof. He moved away, and only rarely was in touch with his son although he did make sure the child support payments were there the first of each month.

No one around Melanie including her friends, her parents and even her son, could understand why she was so depressed over the divorce. They thought she should be relieved. In a way she was, but she was also sad, regretful, and a ton of other emotions. She realized that everyone would have shown a heck of a lot more sympathy and empathy if Michael would have died instead of just leaving.

Because midlife divorce is similar to dealing with the death of a loved one, it is likely that you will go through the similar stages of grief that Dr. Elisabeth Kübler-Ross the well-known psychiatrist and author of the groundbreaking book "On Death and Dying" pioneered in the 1960s. These stages include denial, anger, bargaining, depression, and acceptance.

Although you may not go through every single stage, it is helpful to recognize these stages of grief and know that it is a normal part of the recovery and healing process, both when dealing with a death or the death of a marriage.

THE STAGES OF GRIEVING A DIVORCE

Denial

"This is not really happening to me."

"This is all just a big misunderstanding."

"Maybe he only cheated the one time, and it really didn't mean anything."

"He'll realize he made a mistake and then he'll beg to come back."

"He will get over his midlife crisis and we will work it out."

Anger and Resentment

"How could he even think of doing this to me?"

"All those years of me putting up with him, and he has the audacity to leave?"

"I don't deserve this pain."

"It is so unfair!"

"He thinks he wants a divorce, I'll give him a divorce and make him pay!"

Bargaining

"Please stay, I promise I'll change."

"We will do it your way, I will be better."

"I'll just pretend everything is okay, and it will be."

"If I lose weight, change my hair, and dress nicer, he'll come back."

"I'll start dating again right away, to prove I'm desirable."

Depression

"I don't know how to get over him."

"I simply can't bear the thought of losing him."

"My life is over."

"Women over 40 never are able to find anyone else."

"I'll never find anyone like him again, so what is the point."

"I'm staying home ... everyone will be married at that function anyhow."

Acceptance

"Okay, it happened, I now need to concentrate on myself."
"My marriage is over because it just wasn't good for him or me."
"I am ready to move on with my life."
"My marriage is over, but my life isn't."

Understanding the different stages is an important step to understanding divorce recovery. The important thing is to acknowledge the signs of normal grieving and knowing how to stop that grief from sinking you into a black hole of depression.

Everyone is different, and you may not experience each stage in this exact order or you may stay in one stage longer than another. It is possible, and even likely, to bounce around through the stages depending on the day. Everyone will eventually make it to the acceptance stage which is where you will be ready to move past the pain of your midlife divorce and focus on the wonderful opportunity of creating your new life.

• • •

Here are some important questions you can ask yourself to determine what stage you are in right now:

Are You in Denial?

"This is not happening."
"This is just a phase and everything will be back to normal."
"My divorce is final, but there is a chance that maybe my husband will come back."

While no one can really predict the future, if you want to get over the pain, it is important to accept your current reality. Your X is gone. Your marriage is officially over. Those are harsh statements, but it is time you face reality. If you don't face the reality of your situation you will never be able to look forward to a better future.

You need to stop fighting the facts and denying what truly exists in the present. Granted, your present situation may not be what you had planned on for this stage in your life, but it is what it is. Once you see the situation for what it really is — you are divorced or going to be divorced soon — it will help you open up your mind up to recognize new opportunities and adventures.

Are You Angry?
"I hate my X!"
"I hate him and I really hate his new woman!"
"I hate all men in general!"
"Men are all the same — no good!"
"I hope my X gets hit by a bus!"

Let all the feeling of anger out, especially during the early stages after your decision to divorce. It will give you something outside of yourself to focus on. However, too much anger and staying angry for too long can be self-defeating. You need to learn to figure out if that anger has already outlasted its usefulness.

To find out if your anger has outlasted its usefulness:

Step 1: *Ask yourself the following questions:*
• Do I want to always feel this way?
• How is this anger affecting my personal relationships with the other people in my life?
• Is anger going to help become a better person?
• Will anger help me attract other people?

Step 2: Review your answers.
Once you have acknowledged when anger no longer serves its purpose, you will most likely go on to deal with another phase of the healing process.

Are Your Striking Bargains?
"If he will only come back, I am willing change!"
"I'm on a new diet — I'm going to lose 30 pounds, then he will find me irresistible and will come running back."

"God, if you just put things back to normal and have him come home, I promise to never nag again."

It is also normal to find yourself striking certain deals with your X, with God, and even with yourself. This is an understandable way of getting past a very hurtful situation.

However, no matter how desperately you want to change your situation, you simply have to deal with it and recognize the opportunity to grow through it. If you are truly convinced that bargaining will work for both your best interests, then go for it. Come up with the best deal and pitch it. Should it work, then that's great, but if it doesn't, you need to let go immediately.

Remember, that you should only make changes to yourself for yourself, and not for others. You should embrace change and growth — but for the right reasons and on your own terms.

Are You Depressed?

"I don't want to go out of bed and deal with life anymore."
"What is the point, nothing ever goes my way anyhow."
"Life is too hard, why bother?"

If you are feeling depressed or suicidal, and you do not believe you can pull yourself out of it, then it is highly recommended that you put this book down right now, pick up the phone and call your doctor and insist on being seen today.

Your doctor will help to identify next steps — either recommending medicine and/or therapy. There is no reason in this day and age to suffer through depression. There are many effective drugs and therapies available to you, and do not hesitate if you need them.

If you feel your depression is less severe and you feel up to trying to pull yourself out of it, then the best step to get yourself out of your funk is to know how exactly it benefits you.

To go from blue to better:

Step 1: Ask yourself these questions:

• Is being down and depressed helping you win sympathy?

- Is it your way of showing your X you can't live without him?
- Has it become a habit?

Step 2: Now that you understand what the depression is actually doing for you, tell yourself:

"I am strong, I don't need pity."

"I am worthy of a man who truly wants to be with me and who I really want to be with."

"I refuse to give my X the power over my emotions."

Step 3: Repeat these mantras throughout the day. Put them on sticky notes around your house to remind you that you that you are strong and capable of moving on past this divorce.

!! *Although you may or may not go through every single stage, it is helpful to recognize the stages of grief and know that each stage is a normal part of the recovery and healing process, both when dealing with a death or the death of a marriage.*

GRIEVE THE DEATH OF YOUR MARRIAGE

Midlife divorce will leave you resentful, hurt, drained and raw some days all at the same time. Feelings of hurt, anger, sadness, betrayal, guilt, fear and others may come up and smack you in the face — sometimes when you least expect it. It is important when these feelings come up that you don't repress them. Repressing them will only push the feelings back inside, leaving them to fester and eat you up.

Lynn's husband Jim called her at work from his office to let her know that he was moving out. At first Lynn didn't really understand what Jim was talking about; they had just spent a very nice weekend together visiting their oldest son and his family. Jim had to finally come right out and say that he wanted a divorce before Lynn actually grasped what the conversation was really about. Jim explained that he called at work because he wasn't sure how she would react and he didn't want to deal with it. He informed her that he was headed home to pack up his things, and that he would appreciate it if she just stayed at work.

Lynn hung up the phone, and she went about business as usual. Lynn had always prided herself in not bringing any of her personal problems to the work place. She believed that as the head of a department, she needed to set an example, so no one in her office would have guessed that she was just informed, out of the blue, that her 30 year marriage just ended.

For weeks Lynn continued to live as if Jim was just away on a lengthy business trip. Even when her son called to check in on her after Jim had called to inform him of the divorce, Lynn assured him there was nothing to worry about, and that he shouldn't be worried or upset, because she wasn't. She was a grown woman, and could handle this, and she would be fine.

Lynn never took the time to actually process how awful it had been for her husband to tell her he was leaving her by phone. She never acknowledged how bad she was feeling or how angry and upset she actually was. Instead she put on a 'happy face' and would tell people that 30 years was a long time to be married, so it was time to go their separate ways. The problem was Lynn said this, but really didn't believe it.

Six months after the divorce papers were finalized Lynn went to the doctor for a chronic stomach ache and exhaustion. She was diagnosed with an ulcer. Her doctor insisted that not only did she treat the ulcer, but that she also take a look at her emotional health.

Through her doctor's recommendation Lynn joined a divorce recovery group where she learned to open up. In addition, she also read a lot of books on how to handle emotions. Lynn finally broke down and cried. She cried not only for the loss of her marriage, but also the loss of the image of the man she had been married to, and the loss of the future that they would not share together.

Today, Lynn's reaction to that call would have been much different. Instead of stuffing her emotions inside and pretending everything was all right, she would know how to express them.

It may be a difficult process, but you need to allow yourself to feel these feeling and acknowledge it as a normal reaction. Whenever a feeling comes up, don't hesitate to reach in and grab a hold of as much of the feeling as you can. Allow the feelings to flow through you and out of you. Feel the feelings and then let it go.

By all means, cry if you want. Let the pain and hurt come to you and let it go. By letting yourself feel, you will not only heal the hurt that triggered that moment, you also heal the hurts from your past. Each time, you will gain a little more peace of mind.

If you find that you are crying at all times of the day and night, it may be helpful to put into to place the Fifteen Minute Release.

Instructions for the Fifteen Minute Release:

First of all, not everyone agrees that this methodology is sound. Some will argue that it is ludicrous to try to stop your emotions and hold them aside until a certain 'scheduled' time of day. That is reasonable; however, this is an effective exercise to help with eliminating the constant onslaught of emotions throughout the day. Try it. As with all the exercises in this book, only continue using it if it works for you!

Step 1: Set aside a fifteen minute block of time during the day in which you plan to 'let it all out.'

Step 2: Set the clock for fifteen minutes.

Step 3: During this scheduled time you can let the pain come up, cry until you are blue in the face, and curse your X if you want, but only for fifteen minutes.

Step 4: Practice daily for as long as you feel it is necessary.

If you implement the Fifteen Minute Release you will most likely find that not only will you not be bursting into tears throughout the day as much as before, but that you will actually be done releasing your pain and sadness before the fifteen minutes are up.

If you practice this each day, after a week or so, you will be watching the clock to see if the time is up yet. As you go through different phases of the divorce recovery, whenever you go through a particularly emotional period such as a holiday or anniversary, just reinstate the Fifteen Minute Release back into your daily routine.

You may assume that once the divorce papers are signed, sealed and delivered that you will have reached the acceptance stage and have fully moved on from your midlife divorce. Despite the months or years leading to the actual divorce decree that may give you time to prepare yourself for your life ahead, all too often, you are likely to experience strong waves of feelings all over again once the divorce papers are finalized.

Remember to give yourself time to mourn the death of your marriage. It does not matter who decided to call it quits, or who is more at fault or how long it has been since the decision to divorce was made, it is perfectly normal to grieve over the promise of that relationship.

!! Let the pain and hurt come to you and let it go. By letting yourself feel, you will not only heal the hurt that triggered that moment, you also heal the hurts from your past.

10 TIPS FOR MANAGING YOUR EMOTIONAL NEEDS

TIP #1: Start treating yourself right.
– Get a little more sleep by going to bed early.
– Treat yourself to a massage or take a hot bath.
– If you are tired, and you can, take a nap.
– Get your favorite take-out tonight and eat it while watching your favorite movie.

TIP #2: Be more active.

– Engage in more activities and try to get in some exercise. Get up and get moving — you will feel better.

– Even a short walk each day will help to manage your stress level and release pent-up energy which will keep your emotions on an even keel.

TIP #3: Avoid dwelling on things you can't control.

– When you face certain situations that are simply beyond your control, learn to simply let go. Everyone knows that is usually easier said than done, so start small and try to at least let it go for the moment.

– Below is an exercise to determine if you should handle a situation or let it go. This exercise will give you an easy to implement way to determine if a situation warrants your actions or involvement. It is so easy that you can utilize it throughout your day, spending only a minute or two. Once you get accustomed to utilizing this exercise, you will find that you will stop dwelling on things that you cannot control.

Exercise:

STEP 1: Ask yourself, "Is there anything I can do in this situation?"

If the answer is **YES**, then take the time to write down action steps for what you need to do.

If the answer is **NO**

1. Take a deep, calming breath and prepare yourself to accept whatever will be.

2. After you exhale say out loud or to yourself, "I'm letting this go for now."

TIP #4: Set your expectations.

– Learn the difference between being pessimistic and preparing yourself for a worst-case scenario.

EXAMPLE WORST CASE SCENARIO: Not having enough money to pay the mortgage.

Preparing: Using the money you had saved to buy a new car, get the old one fixed instead. Then put the balance in your savings account to use when needed.

Pessimistic: Thinking, "I will never again own a new car."

TIP #5: Avoid making hasty decisions.

– Do not decide on important things especially if you are still overly emotional.

– If you need guidance, talk it through with family and friends or seek professional help.

TIP #6: Go through the entire process.

– Recognize and feel all the positive and negative emotions, but don't allow your emotions to take over your life or influence the decisions you make.

– While it is important to work through the stages of grief, you do not want to let yourself wallow in any stage too long.

– It is important that you learn to let go of the past and focus on the future. Finding a life coach to help you focus on your goals is highly recommended.

TIP #7: Distract yourself.

– Consider finding or taking up a new hobby or activity that has nothing to do with your X, your marriage or your divorce.

– Take an evening class at the local college.

– Take an online course in a subject that interests you.

– Go back to a hobby or activity you liked doing before you were married.

– Start the small business you always dreamed of having someday.

TIP #8: Have fun.

– Become more involved with activities and people around you.

– Go out with your friends.

– Enjoy a weekend at the park.

– Watch a funny movie.

– Spend time with your children.

NOTE: It really is okay for you to have fun!

TIP #9: Give yourself time to heal.

– No one expects you to bounce back from your midlife divorce right away.

– Focus on yourself and give yourself enough time to truly heal.

– When you need alone time, say so.

TIP #10: Set your sights on the future.

– Despite what happened, always keep in mind that everything happens for a reason.

– Your future is waiting for you to define and live it!

!! It is important to take steps to manage your emotional needs before, during and after a midlife divorce. This will enable you to better handle the additional post-divorce stressors that come your way!

GETTING SUPPORT FROM YOUR EMOTIONAL RESCUE SQUAD

When it comes to seeking support, there are a number of great people in your life you can always run to. However, while these people may always be readily available and genuinely care, they may not always be the best people to talk to when dealing with divorce issues.

Seeking Professional Help

Friends and family are always willing to provide support in any type of crisis. Without a doubt, they will be able to provide you different perspective and practical advice. However, in divorce situations, you may need support from a trained professional such as a therapist or life coach. Equally important is to select the right type of professional to work with for your situation.

Therapists treat medical disorders such as anxiety, depressive disorders, addiction and phobic disorders. They help you better understand your past in order for you to move forward. If you feel that your emotions are out of control or you may fall into one of the disorders listed above, then it is best to search out a trained therapist.

Life Coaches on the other hand work together with 'highly-functioning' people. The assumption is that you are in good mental health, but you need some direction.

A Coach will help you to implement effective strategies to:

- **Build confidence and self-esteem.**
- **Remove self-doubt.**
- **Feel confident when meeting new people.**
- **Build effective relationships.**
- **Develop listening skills.**
- **Get through tough times.**
- **Build stronger bonds.**
- **Improve communication skills.**
- **Identify dreams and acknowledge achievements.**
- **Set compelling goals.**
- **Learn to have more fun in life.**
- **Have more energy.**
- **Find purpose.**

Coaching doesn't focus on why things are what they are, but focuses on what can happen now. It shifts issues and challenges into desired goals. Coaching looks ahead, and not at your past.

Getting professional help, especially before, during and after a midlife divorce, will be of help to you whether you choose to explore your past with a therapist or set new goals for your new life with a life coach.

Below are some examples of how professional help can be quite different from the emotional support you get from your friends and family:

• How Negative Emotions are Handled

Family and friends often address divorce grief with the need to 'fix' the emotion by cheering you up or soothing away any negative emotions. While "don't feel sad" can help you calm down, it does not provide any long-term help.

• Acknowledging the Past is the Past

There's a tendency when seeking support from families and friends to bring up past situations and your marital history since they are familiar with what happened. Unfortunately, this can keep you stuck in replaying the same 'story' over and over again, keeping you living in the past instead of putting more focus on the future, and your self-improvement goals.

• Freedom to Share

There are certain things that you can't discuss with family and friends. Most times, you simply don't want to reveal too much detail to your friends and family. Since professionals are detached from your personal situation, you may be more comfortable confiding in one.

• They Listen

Professionals are specifically trained to listen without judging. Sometimes, you may feel the need to talk, and talk for a full hour, without the fear of being judged or without any advice or without having to deal with an "I-told-you-so" attitude.

!! Therapists treat medical disorders and help you better understand your past. Life Coaches work with people in good mental health, and they don't focus on why things are what they are, but focus on what can happen now.

Seeking Support from Fellow Divorcees

When you are dealing with coming to terms with the finality of your divorce, it can be a comfort to talk to people who have also been in that situation you are in right now. Healing from the trauma of a midlife divorce in isolation can be extremely difficult, and the stress can cause health issues.

It can be quite reassuring to be with people who truly understand the painful process you are going through, as well as the lifestyle changes that a midlife divorce creates. Sharing your story and listening to others who are going through the same thing may help you move along the healing process.

Important considerations for support groups:

• Therapy Group vs. Support Group

Professional therapist-supervised therapy groups usually have an attendance requirement and a fee to join. An alternative is a support group that is led by community volunteers or church leaders and these groups are often free with an open attendance policy.

• Online or Live

There are a multitude of support groups available both online and locally.

Online support will give you the convenience of attending right from your computer in your own home. Online you will find many different groups available so you can then decide which one works for you. In addition, there is the anonymity factor as well as the convenience.

If you are more of a people-person or would like to meet some new friends, then joining a live support group just may be the thing for you. There may not be as many choices, but it is worth the effort to look around. Look in your newspaper, check the internet for websites, and even call some of your local churches and synagogues.

• Philosophy

Are you seeking a support group with a religious orientation or a certain viewpoint?

It is important not to immediately rule out an organization because of an affiliation. For example you most likely will still get a lot out of attending a meeting that is run by Catholics at the local Catholic Church, even though you are Baptist or Jewish or even an atheist. Most divorce recovery groups concentrate on the divorce recovery process and not so much the religious aspects.

However, if your desire is to get into a religious oriented divorce recovery group, you will need to get additional clarification on the group's philosophy upfront so you can make sure you attend the right type of meeting for you.

If you decide a live meeting is a better choice the following should also be considered:

• Size

You need to choose a group size that will not intimidate you. You may also want one that can provide you the attention you need. On the other hand, if you prefer anonymity, a large group may be a better choice; it's entirely up to you.

• Women Only or Mixed Company

Choosing a co-ed group may provide you an opportunity to get a male perspective in a controlled environment. However, for women, it has the ability to backfire.

The purpose of a support group is to nurture, listen and provide a shoulder to cry on. Women in divorce recovery are in a vulnerable state, and so you may find yourself being attracted to one of the men that are in the group based on the fact that it is nice to have a man who is willing to listen and 'understands.' This could lead you to date before you are ready.

Before you think that you were just insulted, think about it. If you choose a co-ed support group and find yourself heading down a path with one of the men in the group, please remember what you just read.

On the other hand, an exclusive female group may provide you the nurturing and understanding you may need at this time, but in an environment where you are free to be yourself and where it will give you time to heal.

• Location
Choose a group that is relatively close and accessible. This will improve the likelihood that you will attend the meetings.

• Frequency
Some support groups meet once a month or once a week, so choose a group that best meets your needs.

The bottom line is to do some research, attend a meeting or two — online or off — and see what feels right for you. If one group doesn't work, then try another.

!! Sharing your story and listening to others who are going through the same thing may help you move along the healing process.

Seeking Support from the 'Right' Friends
When faced with all the changes that come with a midlife divorce, it is also often quite difficult to find someone you can confide in.

The great thing about being a woman is the fact that we are usually surrounded by girlfriends. As one wise woman once said, "Friends are like bras: close to your heart and there for support."

All throughout life, from elementary school through high school, college and beyond, a woman can usually rely on her friends in times of crises.

Most women tend to have a solid support system of friends they can utilize during and after their divorce process; however, an important fact is that having good friends around may not necessarily mean they are all capable of offering the right kind of support you need.

Below are the types of friends that you should keep on your speed dial:

• A friend who is always available for cocktails (or cupcakes) no matter what time of day.

• Friends who start to call and email you the moment they hear about your divorce to see what they can do for you.

• Friends who are intelligent and creative who won't hesitate to speak their minds.

• Friends who will invite you to weekends at the beach or dinners during the week.

• Friends who also have been through a divorce who can give you their 'been-there-done-that-and-lived-through-it' advice.

• Friends who are good listeners and always available when you need to talk to someone.

• Friends, who will remind you of all your good qualities, remind you that he was a fool to leave you, and most importantly ... that you are better off without him. Even if you don't yet buy all of this quite yet — it is sure nice to hear it.

On the other hand, below are possible 'friends' that maybe you should stay away from for a while:

• A friend who wants to rush you back into the single scene.

• Friends who start to call and email you the moment they hear about your divorce just to satisfy their curiosity.

• Friends who seem a little too enthused that you are getting a divorce.

• Friends who never invite you to weekends at the beach or dinners during the week.

• Friends who also have been through a divorce, but are stuck and believe their divorce "ruined their lives."

• Friends who call to say they are checking in, but then within twenty seconds have switched the topic to themselves.

• Friends who like to gossip. This is especially dangerous if the gossip includes your X.

!! While most friends mean well, all too often, they can exacerbate the situation with their misguided attempts to provide the support they think you need. It is therefore important to know and choose carefully the type of friends you choose to surround yourself with.

<u>**SIDE NOTE**</u>: Don't use your children as your support network, even if they are adults and you consider them your friend. Keep boundaries in place. You are still the parent and they are the child, even if they are grown. You would not want to jeopardize the relationship with your children by inadvertently mentioning things that they don't need to know. Remember that your X is also their father. It may be tempting, but it puts them in an unfair position, so reach out to your other friends, or a professional, for support.

CHAPTER VI:
WHAT DOESN'T KILL YOU
MAKES YOU STRONGER

"You can learn to be brave."

You have now learned a little about navigating through the stages of divorce grief and the importance of having a strong support system in place, as well as practical tips for handling your emotions during your divorce recovery.

This chapter will help to motivate you to move forward from your divorce by addressing the courage to face and embrace uncomfortable situations, finding hope, and includes an exercise on flexing your courage muscle.

CULTIVATING COURAGE

Undoubtedly, a midlife divorce is a challenge. It may even be the biggest challenge you face in your life.

What is courage when it comes to a midlife divorce?

In general, it's the ability to keep moving forward with your life, facing each challenge head-on, regardless of the fear you feel. It is about being uncomfortable, pushing through your emotions, and doing it anyway.

Unfortunately, there would be no courage without fear; however, being courageous is managing that fear to the best of your ability, and then taking the most appropriate action that is available to you. Just like most things in life, having courage is something that you can actually practice in order to get good at — the more you practice the better prepared you will be in life to not use fear as an excuse to move forward.

If you are reading this book, you have already shown great courage in your life because you have faced your midlife divorce head-on and are willing to face the next chapter in your life as an independent woman rewriting your new 'happily ever after.'

• • •

Below is an exercise to help you further strengthen your courage muscle. This is a lengthier exercise, and may take weeks to complete, but it will be well worth the effort. Once you finish even one item from Step 4, you will feel that you can face any challenge because you will realize that in most cases, it is fear that keeps you stuck.

Be courageous and take the time to complete this exercise!

<u>**Exercise:**</u>

STEP 1: Get out a piece of paper and a pen or pull up a blank document on your computer.

STEP 2: Make a list of all the things that you're afraid to do, but wish you weren't.

These can be something big like starting your own business, to something smaller such as eating at a restaurant alone.

STEP 3: Put that list in order from least fearful to most fearful.

STEP 4: Starting today, start working on this list. Start at the top and work your way down.

To Help in Completing Step 4 Try the Following:

• **Accept the fact that there will be some fear involved in completing the list.**

Remember that fear can be decreased, but sometimes not completely eliminated.

Remember that living courageously means moving forward regardless of the fear you feel.

• **Make a decision that you are going to conquer your fear.**

Once you declare to yourself that you're going to tackle your fears one at a time, you have eliminated any other possibilities, and it will help you to complete this step.

• **Ask yourself, "What's the worst that can happen?"**

Many times what we imagine is much worse than the reality.

• **Tell yourself repeatedly that fear isn't a good excuse to avoid doing something.**

Unless you're going to drive off of a mountain, being afraid is not an effective way of choosing your course of action.

• **Recognize that feelings of fear and excitement are similar.**

It can be a very thin line that separates the two for most people. Think about riding a roller coaster or seeing a horror movie. Since it is difficult to recognize the difference, just tell yourself you're just really excited as you move through your list.

• **Reward yourself.**

After you complete an item on your list, give yourself something special, such as renting your favorite movie or buying a new book, and remember to tell yourself, "good job", be proud. It is very difficult to face your fears and conquer them.

• **Use all the tools you can tap into as you make your way
through your list**.

Such as: Faith, meditation, hypnosis, and prayer.

Once you have completed this exercise, congratulate yourself. You faced your fears, conquered activities you once thought you would never be able to do. You *are* courageous!

• • •

It's important to remember that every day gives you another opportunity to succeed. Pursuing your happiness can only be done one step at a time. Be courageous. Once you take the first step, the ones that follow seem to fall into place.

> *Below are just some of the ways I have flexed my courage muscle since my divorce:*
> • *Started my own business.*
> • *Wrote this book.*
> • *Went up on stage and sang at a Karaoke bar.*
> • *Passed my master certification in life coaching.*
> • *Published multiple articles.*
> • *Became a bocce scorer for the Senior Olympics*
> • *Attended a rap concert with my daughter.*
> • *Drove from Raleigh NC to Niagara Falls, Canada*
> • *Co-authored a book.*
> • *Started my own website.*
> • *Learned hypnosis.*
> • *Joined two professional women's organizations.*
> • *Danced in a flash mob.*
> *Every day I try to be courageous in everything I do. That intent helps me to live the life I want to live, under my own terms. I know that sometimes I am not going to feel comfortable or competent in a situation, but I also know that if I face those feelings and do it anyway — life can be wonderful!*

!! Being courageous is all about taking action in spite of fear, not the absence of fear, so continue to cultivate your courage today!

FINDING HOPE IN YOUR LIFE

After a midlife divorce it may seem impossible to have hope; however, it is not only possible, but it is a necessity in order to move on and live the life you want to live.

Remember ... no matter how hopeless things may appear right now, you have the power to change things for the better. This includes not only the challenging circumstances that may have resulted from your midlife divorce, but includes changing how you personally feel for the better. To do this you must embrace the idea of having hope.

Start Small

To start feeling more hopeful today, try remembering some of the things you've accomplished in your life. Don't just remember the larger accomplishments such as having a baby or landing that promotion, but also remember the seemingly smaller things such as learning to drive a car.

To help to remind you what you have achieved in your life, try this simple exercise. The exercise below is a quick and easy way to remind you that sometimes the seemingly impossible is, in fact, possible.

Exercise:

STEP 1: Sit back and relax in a comfortable chair.

STEP 2: Mentally list at least 15 things you have accomplished in your life.

In doing this exercise you will be reminded that you have already faced and accomplished many different things in your life that at one time seemed impossible.

Optimism

Another way in which you can start being more hopeful is by trying to be more optimistic about life. We all know those people, the ones who persistently see the bright and sunny side of things. They're the ones that could stand in the middle of a raging hurricane, with the wind blowing the roofs off of houses, and they would say, "I think it's starting to clear up."

If you are not naturally one of these people, you may have the urge to whack them right in the face; however, as you work through your divorce recovery, you really need to seek out these optimistic people and spend time with them. The reason is that their optimism will soon start to rub off on you, and if you talk to them about your personal challenges; they most likely will have a new and more positive perspective that can really give you a push in the right direction.

Think about it: negative people accomplish nothing. They criticize others' efforts, but do nothing themselves that could possibly garner criticism. These are the last people in the world you want to be around. Seek out the optimists; even emulate the optimists, as they provide the good sense needed to complete any task, regardless of its size.

Interesting Activities

Another action to take when trying to be more hopeful is to do activities that inspire you. This can include embracing your faith by going to your place of worship or exploring your spiritual side. Try watching children play or reading an inspiring book. One very effective way to become more hopeful about life is by volunteering to help the homeless or hospice patients. This will definitely show you that things aren't quite as challenging for you as you originally thought and it will give you a different perspective on your midlife divorce situation.

Nature

Try spending more time in nature. Just looking around — the birds, the trees, the butterflies — will remind you of what's good in life. It will remind you that although you may not be able to create a mountain, you too are capable of remarkable things.

So, to reiterate, if you want to find hope in your life, you always can by doing the following:

• **Remember your achievements.**
• **Surround yourself with optimistic people.**
• **Try activities that inspire you.**
• **Spend more time in nature.**

Although your search for hope will take some work, especially after a midlife divorce, the bottom line is to never give up and you'll soon discover that you have plenty of reasons to be hopeful.

One last thought: Hope is a state of mind. The only place that you need to search for it is the six-inch space between your ears.

!! *To find the hope in your life, remember the things you have already achieved; surround yourself with optimistic people, participate in inspiring activities and spend more time in nature.*

MOVE FORWARD IN YOUR LIFE

In order to live a full and complete life, we must learn how to let go of past failures and disappointments and not carry them with us into our future, and this is especially true after a midlife divorce.

Don't get stuck in the drama of your marriage and divorce. Hanging on to pain, bitterness and disappointment from your past can be a heavy burden to carry. It will affect your moods, attitudes, relationships, career and basically all aspects of your life.

In the next chapter you will learn how to let go in order to move into the life you want to live!

CHAPTER VII:
LET GO OF YOUR PAST,
EMBRACE YOUR FUTURE

"Letting go is easier said, than done."

Now that you understand the grieving stages of divorce a little better, and have started to flex your courage muscle, it is now time to look at finding the path to happiness and health after your midlife divorce. The key here is that it is not about adding something more to your life, but actually the act of removing — letting go.

In this chapter you will learn why you need to let go of your X, your dysfunctional habits, and your limiting beliefs, as well as stepping outside of your comfort zone. By following the tips and exercises in this chapter you'll be on your way in the divorce recovery process.

In order to move in this new direction, you need to get rid of your old map. This would include emotions, beliefs, possessions, and other 'baggage' that may be holding you back or worse, pointing you in the wrong direction.

To get yourself pointed in the RIGHT direction, and to make room for wonderful things to come into your life, you need to learn to **LET GO**.

THE FEAR OF LETTING GO

Letting go is frightening for a number of reasons.

The first is change. People generally do not like change. For example, even if you had an unhappy marriage, and your life was far from ideal, you knew what to expect. You didn't mind staying married, rather than face a major change.

The second is fear of the future. The future, by definition, is unknown. This causes some people a lot of stress. This is especially true after a midlife divorce because your future is going to be drastically different than the one you had envisioned while married. For this reason, the fear of your future is usually exaggerated.

Third is fear of losing the important things and people in your life. Divorce will force you to make sacrifices of not only material possessions you have accumulated in your marriage or even the marital home, but it will also force certain relationships and friendships to end.

The important point to remember is that if you refuse to face these fears of letting go, you will not be able to know your deepest self, aspire to your life goals or even know who your real friends are.

!! Change, fear of the future and losing possessions or relationships are three fears that need to be faced when letting go and moving on.

LETTING GO OF THE X

While it is commonly recommended to maintain a civil relationship with your X, it is also important to set and maintain boundaries. In order for you to truly move on to your new life, it is critical that you learn to fully disengage yourself from any emotional, physical and even financial dependency with your X.

As a reminder, this guide was written with the assumption that your children are older, in their late teens or adults. Understandably, letting go of the X is a lot more complex if you still have younger children and child custody issues to deal with; however, even then you can benefit by implementing some strong boundaries.

Not letting go of your X will prevent you from growing and moving on with your life. You need to view your X as just that — an **X**. He is now part of your history — your past — and you do not live in the past!

Below are some of the important reasons why you need to let go of the X:

REASON 1: **It is difficult to get past the pain and the reality that comes with divorce if you choose to stay fixated on your X, your marriage and your divorce.**

You need to let go of your X's emotional hold over you. This means having only necessary contact with your X during your divorce recovery. There is no need to rehash the problems in your marriage and why he said or you said this or that. Staying emotionally fixated will only keep you from truly moving forward with your new life.

REASON 2: **By letting go of the X, you will be able to focus on reconnecting with yourself emotionally.**

The divorce should mean your X is now nothing more than an acquaintance. There is no need to tell him anything about your life.

Once you accept this fact, his presence in your life and the importance you gave him will no longer be front-and-center. This will give your mind the space it needs to achieve complete clarity — emotional and logical.

Choosing to keep in touch with your X will definitely slow down your healing process. If you fail to focus on yourself, you will never know what you really need in order to fully heal and move on.

REASON 3: **The act of letting your X go will help you avoid the habit of idealizing your marriage or your X.**

When you are suffering the pain of a divorce, it is all too easy to latch on to the memory of all the good times and overlook the bad times of your marriage. You forget the fighting or the infidelity or the hurt. You view your marriage as if it were a constant vacation.

The same goes for idealizing your X. All of a sudden you forget all his imperfections and choose to put him on a pedestal. It is important to remember that no one is perfect — neither you nor your X — and all of this idealization will make you emotionally unavailable for new and healthy relationships.

REASON 4: **By letting go of your X, the temptation to have sex with him will be removed.**

It's quite common for some couples to have sex even after the divorce papers have been signed because it is easy and familiar.

Having sex with the X is sometimes done to soothe loneliness or to re-live the feeling of being a couple again. Also, as you know, women are at their sexual peak at midlife. The X is familiar, and can be seen as someone to satisfy your needs. This is a very bad idea! The comfort and pleasure you may get from getting together with your X will not be worth the emotional price you will pay.

You are merely using a band aid to cover a gaping emotional wound. This will not fix your loneliness and you will not feel like a couple again because you are *not*.

Allowing your X back into your life means making yourself vulnerable again to the pain and frustration and all the other emotions you suffered during your marriage and your divorce.

Having sex with the X not only delays your healing, it also leaves you at high risk of deep and lasting emotional scarring.

So, what's a girl to do? The answer is *anything* but having sex with the X. You are now single, or about to be, you are attractive, have lots of options, and have an active imagination. Use it. Of course certain solo activities do not replace the intimacy of having real sex, but it is an emotionally and physically responsible thing to do for yourself during your divorce recovery because the bottom line is this: It is *never* a good idea to have sex with the X.

REASON 5: **By letting go of your X during your divorce recovery you will lay the groundwork for the possibility of becoming friends, or at least somewhat friends, in the future.**

It can be tempting to stay friends right away, proving how 'modern and evolved' you are, especially if the divorce was somewhat amicable.

Unfortunately, the decision to remain close friends immediately will make it more difficult to heal, so it is highly recommended severing all but essential communications during the healing process.

Now, it can be possible to establish friendship later on if that is what *you* want, but only when you have completely let go of the relationship of husband and wife, and any thoughts of you two as a couple.

REASON 6: **Letting go of your X will allow you to heal any self-doubt and negativity you are harboring, and will give you the chance to work on a more positive outlook.**

Marriages usually end because what is broken can no longer be fixed. If you cling to your X, you may decide it is an easier path to go back and accept the broken relationship. This will only result in your self-esteem going down the drain along with any respect you may have for yourself.

REASON 7: **You need to let go of your X if you ever hope to find a new relationship — one that may be better for you.**

Going through a midlife divorce does not mean that your relationship days are over; quite the contrary. Once you start paying attention, you'll be amazed by what you find.

However, if you refuse to cut all the emotional ties with your X, you may consciously hold on to the notion that 'he is the one' or 'he was my only one true love.' This will prevent you from taking notice of other people and exploring the possibility of dating.

REASON 8: **You must let go of your X in order to grow from the woman you were before the divorce, into the woman you want to be today ... and tomorrow.**

By choosing to cut the ties, you can focus on trying out new hobbies and activities and enjoy things that you and you alone enjoy. By letting go of the X, you are better prepared to acquire new passion without taking in to consideration what he thinks.

Besides, who cares what he thinks? You are now an independent woman who thinks for herself!

• • •

<u>In order to effectively cut the ties with your X</u>:

• Only communicate with your X when absolutely necessary — having a plumbing problem come up or wondering how to start the lawn mower is *not* an absolute necessity.

• Tell your X, if applicable, that you need to sever the ties for a while, so that you can work on yourself and move on. This is called setting boundaries!

• Invest time in working on your personal development — by reading this book you are already on your way. Continue on and start looking forward to the new you and your new life.

!! If you are no longer in a marriage, why should you give your X any reasons to hold you back?

LETTING GO OF YOUR COMFORT ZONE

Open yourself up to letting go of old habits, ideas and people that are not serving your best interests since your divorce. As you're discovering, life is full of changes. Stepping out of your comfort zone can be stressful, which is why most people choose not to do so by trotting out a series of woeful excuses.

The fact is that a midlife divorce is the perfect opportunity to let go.

Cheryl had spent the last ten years working at a job that had made her a lot of money, but made her miserable. She had just turned 45 this past year, and couldn't help thinking that there had to be more to life. She knew she had to make a career change, so she started to read everything she could get her hands on regarding midlife career changes.

In addition to the job that was draining her life force, she also felt as though her home life was almost as bad, if not worse. For the last four years her husband Tom would come home from work and immediately go onto his computer to play an internet game. He would spend hours playing, while Cheryl busied herself by cleaning the house or watching TV or reading.

Cheryl kept asking herself why she stayed. Unfortunately, she was so drained from her job she didn't have the energy to concentrate on her marital situation, so she just went through the motions.

Cheryl knew from experience that there was little to no chance that Tom would want to talk or go for a walk or go out to dinner or go to a movie or even go to bed at the same time as her. It used to upset her, and she used to argue with Tom about it, but after a while she just gave up because even when he did agree to do something with her he almost acted as if he was in withdrawal. He would get testy and nervous. It was as if he couldn't wait to get back to his computer and his game.

No one really understood the pain this caused Cheryl or how incredibly lonely she was. Whenever she reached out for support from friends and family, they all basically said the same thing, "Well, at least he isn't out drinking, running around on you, or hitting you — and he has a good job." Cheryl didn't really see these as 'benefits,' she knew those qualities would be the minimum she would want in a husband.

After doing a lot of research, career tests, and working with a life coach, Cheryl finally made the decision to quit her job. She then worked on and started her own home-based business providing marketing help to small business owners. Her business took off within the first six months, and she realized that although she was working longer hours than she had been at her corporate job, she felt energized. She loved pulling together products for her clients and she woke up every day looking forward to working on building her business. She felt free and empowered.

As her energy increased, she now was able to take a hard look at her marriage. After a lot of soul-searching, she told Tom that she wanted to talk about their marriage. He wasn't interested in having a lengthy discussion, and after ten minutes he went back to his computer game. As Cheryl went to bed that night, by herself, she knew what she needed to do. She called a lawyer first thing the next morning.

Make no doubt, it isn't easy to step away from people, habits or ideas that you have had for a long time and that are comfortable; however, choosing to cling to the past will prevent you from making the most of your life.

One way to embrace change and help you step out of your comfort zone is when you begin to see the good in every change. You become more comfortable with the idea of change, and start to anticipate the new adventures that lie ahead. With the mindset of finding good in every change, including your midlife divorce, you're then ready, willing, and able to expand your comfort zone.

Try these effective techniques to help you break free of the limits of your comfort zone:

• Think positively.

Instead of thinking about all that could go wrong, think about what could go *right*. Have faith that your divorce is the catalyst — the proverbial kick-in-the-pants — that you needed to start living a new and better life.

• Take small steps.

The journey of a thousand miles begins with? You know the answer. As Confucius pointed out, these steps will add up to something big as long as you keep moving forward.

• Use your imagination.

By thinking the way you always have, you limit your imagination. Some see a rock pile, you see a cathedral. Let your imagination run wild.

• Do something new.

It needn't be exciting or produce great results; just do something you've *never* done before.

Try something you always wanted to try but your X didn't — that restaurant around the corner, or your hair in a new style.

Make it a game. Do something different each day.

• Accept help.

If you ask your friends and family for help, they'll be there for you. Have someone meet you at that new restaurant. Don't be a martyr. Getting help will alleviate your stress while you're expanding your comfort zone.

Don't just limit your help to family and friends — learning from an expert is also something to consider. For example, most local home hardware stores offer free classes on how to do almost any home repair. Stepping out of your comfort zone will not only enable you to learn a new skill, but also build your self-confidence.

• Meet new people.

Take a chance: Strike up a casual conversation with the people around you. You may walk away with a new acquaintance.

A former professional baseball player, Joaquin Andujar, was asked what he thought about his chosen profession. "I can describe baseball in one word — 'You never know'." Indeed ... you never know.

!! Remember that there are no set rules to expanding your comfort zone. Your main goal is to be happy with your life. Don't do anything that you don't want to do; however, if staying within your comfort zone causes you regret then step outside of the zone and grab all the gusto you can out of life!

LETTING GO OF DYSFUNCTIONAL HABITS

Part of the preparation in carving out your new life is to identify your dysfunctional habits. Those acquired while married and/or acquired because of your divorce. While most dysfunctional habits began to provide temporary relief from some sort of pain or suffering, they can subtract years from your life.

They include seemingly innocuous things — skipping meals, not getting enough sleep, obsessively searching the internet for information on divorce — to much more serious habits such as excessive alcohol consumption, smoking, taking stimulants or depressants.

In order to start letting go of these habits, you need to believe — there's that word again — that you are worth the effort. The best way to do that is to substitute better habits. Start taking better care of yourself. Make it a priority. Be the best you that you can be!

LETTING GO OF YOUR LIMITING BELIEFS

What is a limiting belief?

A limiting belief is your very own notion about you that holds you back from reaching your potential.

Our beliefs dictate our behavior, and the behaviors we display over an extended period determine the quality of our lives.

For example, if you believe that you can only work in the career area you've always worked in, you will never attempt to try a different career path.

Another example is if you believe that you will never marry again because you are too old, then you will never put yourself out there and may miss a wonderful new relationship.

This is not about believing in the impossible. To achieve most goals requires a mixture of belief, talent, age and innate intelligence. For example if you want to be a prima ballerina on stage, but have never had a ballet lesson, this is probably unrealistic. However, if you want to take ballet, and believe you are too old to start, this is a limiting belief.

So, the bottom line is that to truly change your life you need to first discover, and then change, some of your limiting beliefs.

Examples of limiting beliefs include:
• Fear of embarrassment
• Guilt
• Resentment
• Remorse
• Most judgments
• Excessive self-induced pressures — all those expressed with 'oughts', 'shoulds', 'musts' and 'have to's'.

Limiting beliefs have a way of coming out, especially after you have experienced something traumatic — like a divorce — and they have a way of hanging around and blocking you from moving ahead with your life.

Try the following exercise; it will help you question your limiting beliefs. This exercise is an easy way to question the beliefs that may be holding you back. The more you question the underlying assumptions of your limiting beliefs, the more success you'll experience in your new life.

Exercise:

STEP 1: Get out a piece of paper and a pen or pull up a blank document on your computer.

STEP 2: Answer the following questions:

• **Which belief do you want to change?**
You need to be able to see it to work with it effectively. Write it down.

For example, one limiting belief is: "I will never have a lot of money."

• What has the belief cost you?

Make a list of all the ways this belief has negatively impacted your life. Really think about it. It helps to have as much negative ammunition as you can muster to get rid of that old belief.

Spend some time; it can even take a couple of days to get a complete list.

For example, using the limiting belief of "I will never have a lot of money," you've most certainly deprived yourself of big-ticket items you wanted to buy.

• What advantages has the belief provided you?

Maybe believing that you could never be wealthy has allowed you to avoid taking risks. Perhaps it has allowed you to work at a profession that's easy for you, but unfulfilling.

It may be hard to figure out what the advantages are, but they exist, so keep thinking.

• What new belief would you like to have as a replacement?

For example, for the belief listed above, a new replacement would be: "I *can* make any amount of money I set my mind to."

Be thoughtful and develop a new belief that will serve you well in the future.

STEP 3: Come up with a list of ways in which the new belief will impact your life, for the better.
- Consider how you would feel.
- What could you become?
- How would your lifestyle change?
- Would it help other people around you?

STEP 4: Think about how you can start demonstrating the new belief today.

Following our wealth-theme, it most likely is not the right time to plan the interior of your new vacation home just yet, but... What could you do right now?

- Make a plan to make more money?
- Start looking for a better paying job?
- Look for ways to invest the money you already have?
- Look for ways to stop spending some of what you now have?

Even a small change can help the process.

STEP 5: Start living your new belief.

It will not be easy at first, but taking the time to complete the steps above will make it easier. Each day, behave as if you've held the new belief all your life.

STEP 6: Repeat with another limiting belief.

Breaking through your limiting beliefs will not only help you with your divorce recovery, but will help you in all areas of your life.

!! *While our behaviors determine the quality of our lives, our beliefs largely determine our behaviors. Beliefs are really the core to everything you do and become.*

CHOOSE PEACE

One important aspect of letting go is the very decision you make to **TRULY LET GO**. To do this you need to consciously choose to be at peace with your marriage, your divorce and your X, as well as your life right now. This will give you the freedom and ability to see the possibilities for a better future.

CHAPTER VIII:
CHANGE YOUR THOUGHTS

"You are a reflection of what you think."

As we learned in the last chapter, it is important to let go of certain people, beliefs and even physical items in order to move on from your midlife divorce; however, it is equally important that you also work on letting go of the negative self-talk that may be holding you back from living the life you want.

This chapter will address how you talk to yourself, what that little voice inside you really is trying to accomplish, and strategies to change the negative self-talk into positive self-talk. This will get you ready to fully embrace the next chapter, Divorce Detox.

NEGATIVE SELF-TALK

How often do you hear yourself say something similar to the following?

"I should have seen it coming."

"I should have known and realized what was happening."

"I wasted all those years of my life."

When you find yourself saying things like this, remind yourself to stay in the present.

Immediately say:

"I am in the right place in my life and at the right time."

"Everything that I have been through in my life has brought me to this point."

"I am where I am supposed to be, right now."

These simple statements can help you stop the negative thought pattern and will remind you that it is time to let go and move on from your past.

Self-talk is a constant in your life. You start talking to yourself when you wake up in the morning and you don't stop until you fall asleep at night. When self-talk is positive and helpful, amazing things can happen. When self-talk is negative, life can be much more challenging than it has to be.

Fortunately, negative self-talk often has very little basis in reality, but if you continue to reinforce the negative self-talk — soon you will not know the difference.

Like much of who you are, your style of self-talk is a habit that has been formed by your experiences and surroundings. Imagine how your life could change for the better if you were able to alter your self-talk into something more supportive and inspiring.

Try the following exercise to monitor your self-talk. This is a simple exercise that will let you quickly see how your negative self-talk may have become a habit that needs to be changed.

Exercise:

STEP 1: Get a small notebook and pen.

STEP 2: Make a list of your negative self-talk phrases and attitudes.

To do this:

For 24 hours, write down everything you say to yourself that isn't supportive, regardless of whether or not you think it's true.

Here are a few examples to get you thinking:

"I'm too old to do that."

"This job will always be a nightmare."

"Things will never get better."

STEP 3: Prioritize your list.

Which items have the greatest negative impact on your life and your sense of happiness?

Put the list in order, from greatest negative impact to least.

Note: Prioritizing is important because it will naturally force you to spend your time on the most important items.

STEP 4: Create a new list.

Now that you've made your list, you're going to improve it. Convert at least the first 5 items on your list into positive thoughts.

If you're feeling motivated, you can rewrite all of them.

Note: Even if you don't believe the new, positive idea, just change it into a positive version.

For example: "I'm too old for that." changes to, "Age is just a number. I can do anything I want to do."

STEP 5: Change your thinking.

Now, for the challenging part, each time you catch yourself engaging in self-talk matching an item from your original list (step 1), substitute the new self-talk expression (step 3).

Be conscientious at all times. Considering how many times you may have said the negative item to yourself, this new practice will require a lot of attention. The good news is that over time, the positive things you say to yourself will become a habit, too!

• • •

Self-talk will always be there, so it benefits you to have some control over it. Anything you hear over and over again, you start to believe. That's just the way our minds work. The first step to gaining that control is to monitor your thoughts, then take the necessary steps to change those negative thoughts to positive ones. As with all habits, these self-talk patterns can be hard to change, but investing the time to try to do so can really boost your happiness.

Have you ever stopped to wonder if your divorce might have amped up your negative self-talk, pushing it into overdrive?

Start to notice…

- How many times you put yourself down.
- How often you compare yourself to others.
- How many times you find fault in what you're doing.
- How often you compromise your values.

Nancy had noticed that since her divorce last year she had started to compare herself to other women. Nancy was 42, and had always felt confident in her looks even though she would definitely not fit the 'magazine model' look that most women strived for.

Nancy was average height and was larger than average both in her bust and her backside. She had never before hidden her curves; in fact, she usually wore clothes that highlighted them. She was bold and confident, but that changed when her long-term marriage fell apart and the divorce happened.

All of a sudden, Nancy's confidence had taken a nose dive. She started to worry about those extra inches, and the fact that she was now over 40. These were two areas that had never concerned her before.

It wasn't until she went out to dinner with her friend that Nancy started to really take notice how she was talking to herself about herself. During the dinner, each time Nancy was critical of herself, her friend hit her glass with her fork. Needless to say, there was a lot of 'clinking' going on during that one hour dinner and it was a real eye-opener for Nancy.

!! *Anything you hear over and over again, you start to believe.*

TRY POSITIVE AFFIRMATIONS

As we have learned, having a negative mindset will hold you back from the life you desire, so it makes sense that developing a positive mindset would be an effective strategy to help you turn your life around after your divorce.

Yes, this is a bit 'new-age,' and the skeptic in you may question if affirmations really will make a difference in your life. The answer is — why not give it a try? It costs nothing and if it doesn't work, you haven't lost anything but a little time. However, if you don't do something about your negative thoughts, the self-pity, the complaining, and the lack of new actions — or, as Dr. Phil calls that entire package: Stinkin' Thinkin' — then you'll never be able to achieve that new future of yours.

Positive affirmations are essentially short, positive thoughts or statements about some outcome that you want to see happen in your life.

The daily repetition of these affirmations has the power to impress the subconscious mind and trigger it into positive action, thereby transforming your habits, behavior, mental attitudes and reactions.

Positive affirmations can help develop a powerful and positive attitude to life, which are essential elements in living a successful and healthy life after your divorce.

To get you started, below are some affirmations. It is also recommended that you create your own, more personalized ones. Always create them in the first person, "I", and state what it is you want as if it has already occurred.

For example: "I am calm under all circumstances."

NOTE: It is recommended you repeat your positive affirmations throughout the day and right before bed.

• • •

Affirmations You Can Use:
"I allow myself out of my comfort zone and appreciate all the rewards that are available to me."
"I allow the feeling of change to create peace in my life."

"I accept new opportunities and embrace the new experiences that come along with it."

"I reignite my passions through self-reflection."

"Change is my friend. It is a gentle reminder that there are greater things in store for me."

"I react well in the presence of chaos."

"I keep only two mental snapshots of myself: where I am and where I want to be in life."

"I am focused on my goals and dreams."

"I accept the faults of others."

"I look at the journey ahead with great peace because I am adaptable and confident."

"I am perfectly whole. I do not need repair."

"The one thing that I have total control over is my attitude."

"I am strong and competent."

"I have no need to worry about the unknown. I enjoy living in the moment."

"Worry and anxiety cannot change my circumstance, only positive thoughts and actions can."

!! *Affirmations are short, positive statements that are written in the present tense. Affirmations describe how you want to feel as if you already experience those positive emotions. Start small and allow the positive results to motivate you to use affirmations more and more in the future.*

Now that you have learned how to get your internal dialogue working in your favor, changing the negative self-talk to positive self-talk, you are now ready to move on to divorce detox.

CHAPTER IX:
DIVORCE DETOX

*"To create space for new experiences,
one needs to clear out the old."*

What is divorce detox?

It is when you realize that the bitterness, blame, resentment, hurt and anger you are carrying around and 'using' every day is causing you misery. It is when you realize that you may have become slightly 'addicted' to these feelings since your midlife divorce, and you now know that in order to start moving on you need to free yourself from these feelings.

In this chapter you will learn to purge those negative emotions and forgive others, including yourself, in order to be happy.

EMOTIONAL DETOX

Bitterness

When you bite into an orange skin, it is bitter. It leaves a bad taste in your mouth.

Bitterness from your midlife divorce is similar. The end of your marriage, the divorce itself, along your X, may have left a bitter taste in your mouth. You may feel hostility and distrust over the situation, which is normal and a result of the severe grief, anguish, and disappointment caused by your midlife divorce.

However, bitterness is the same as taking poison and expecting the other person — most likely your X — to die. The bitterness you hold onto and keep inside only hurts you.

You're going to be angry, thinking about the years of sacrifice that comes with several decades of marriage. It will take time and effort to get past the feeling of hurt, anger and maybe even abandonment. However, at a certain point you need to let go of all of it.

When you have some time to yourself, the following writing exercise may help you get rid of the bitter poison inside that may be keeping you from moving past your midlife divorce.

Exercise:

STEP 1: Get out a paper and pen or pull up a blank document on your computer.

STEP 2: Write a short story on your marriage and divorce *but*, from **the point of view of your X**.

Write as if you were he, and try to see things as you *think* he has seen them during your marriage and the divorce.

The purpose of this exercise is that it may help you gain insight into why your X may have treated you the way he did, and you may gain better insight as to where he was coming from.

This is a simple exercise but it can have profound effects, and it may help release some of the bitter feelings that are eating you up on the inside.

!! *Bitterness is the same as you taking poison and expecting the other person — most likely your X — to die.*

Blame

What is meant by blame?

Blame is when you hold someone else responsible for an action. In this case, it is quite likely that you blame your X for the way your life is today. Blaming him for the trouble in your marriage and also blaming him for the divorce along with every change and every problem that has come up in your life is no way to live.

When talking about a midlife divorce, it may take supernatural powers to stop blaming your X. However, it is important that you understand that you will heal faster if you can stop blaming others for your circumstances and focus instead on your new life.

It may be difficult, but it is time to take responsibility for your circumstances and your life. You need to do this if you want to move forward into your new life and regain your happiness. Thoughts have power, so make them work *for* you, not *against* you.

To do this, take some time to think about the following:

- What did you learn from your marriage?
- What did you learn from your divorce?
- What good things came from your marriage?
- What good things came from your divorce?

Before you state that there were no good things concerning your divorce, stop and think about that. There is always good if you look for it. Most people forget to look for the good that comes in all experiences, and that includes your divorce. For example, a good that has come from your divorce is that it proved you can survive just about anything.

Now, think about this:

- What are you doing today that you are learning from?
- What good things are coming from what is happening in your world right now, today?

Start making it a *top priority* to recognize the learning experience and the good in the things you're doing today. You aren't required to forget the past, but you can move away from it. Living in memories is no longer necessary. Live in the present, and look to the future. It's much easier to see where you're going that way, and that will keep you from blaming a person/situation that is no longer a part of your life.

!! Understand that you will heal faster if you can stop blaming others, including your X, for your circumstances and focus instead on your new life ahead.

Resentment

Resentment is experiencing a negative emotion — usually anger or hatred toward a person as the result of a real or imagined wrongdoing.

It is understandable that emotions may still be raw after your midlife divorce, and resentment may be lingering toward your X. More than likely when you see your X, resentment will rear its ugly head. Look at the progression: resentment, anger, hate. Not a great combination!

You should limit your interactions with your X during your divorce recovery period. There are some occasions — especially if you have children — that will force you to interact. Holidays, graduations, and weddings are just a few of those.

During these times, it is important for your recovery, and for the event itself, that you take the high road.

As much as it is possible, you want to create a comfortable and harmonious atmosphere for everyone, and remind yourself that it is only for a short while. This is a much healthier approach for you, and if you have children, they will be forever grateful that you have made the decision to be the 'better man,' at least for the event.

If you are forced to interact with the X, try keeping the past in the past. No matter what had happened between the two of you during your marriage or your divorce, for the sake of everyone around (including your children) you need to try to create a new dynamic when your X is around. Yes, your family is not what it used to be and may not be what you had envisioned, and you may still resent your X for that fact; however, a holiday or family occasion is *not* the place to vent that resentment.

Below are some tips to help get you through a holiday or family occasion:

TIP #1: Listen to your head not your heart.
Your feelings are still raw, but think before you speak. Try the **Five Seconds Rule** — silently counting to five — before responding to your X or the new woman in his life.

TIP#2: Watch what you say.
It is easy to let the resentment, anger and hatred come out in even 'innocent' sounding sentences.

TIP #3: Use soothing tones and words.
Do not let your X push your buttons. If you think you're being "baited," walk away.

TIP #4: Keep topics neutral.
Try to avoid topics you know will aggravate the X. Don't "bait" him.

TIP #5: Be polite to the new woman, if there is one.
This one is hard, but you can do it! The first time is always the most difficult. After that, it becomes easier.

Now that you understand the importance of letting the old resentments go on those special days, you can also start working on letting the resentments go altogether.

WHY DO WE CHOOSE TO HANG ON TO THE PAIN?

What is the payoff you expect to receive by hanging on to the pain of your midlife divorce?

Let us explore some of the possible reasons we choose to hang on to the pain:

REASON: If you are upset, angry, and sad forever then you may believe you are validating how much your marriage meant to you.

REASON: Clinging to old habits such as over-eating, over-shopping, over-anything proves to you that you are a victim of your circumstance.

REASON: Continually blaming your X, or your divorce, for where your life is now means you don't have to take any responsibility or action. It's much easier to sit in that mud pile because you have an "excuse."

It is time to cut the cord: Let go of the pain, the bitterness, the blame and the resentment. You need to emotionally detox from your marriage and your divorce in order to move forward and have a rewarding life — a happy life. This means facing the (other) F Word — Forgiveness!

FORGIVENESS — IT IS POSSIBLE

Forgiveness isn't about saying that whatever happened during your marriage and during your divorce is irrelevant. Nor does it mean you are condoning inexcusable behavior. It is about you and how forgiving allows you to move on.

WHY YOU NEED TO FORGIVE YOURSELF FIRST

Maybe it was you or your X who had the affair, causing your marriage to implode. Maybe you both drifted so far apart that the marriage couldn't be fixed. Maybe it was you who initiated the divorce in order to live a better life. Whatever the reasons for the divorce, you need to forgive yourself.

You may have already heard the advice that in time, you need to forgive your X, but in order to even consider that possibility, you need to first forgive yourself.

It is all too easy to say, "move on" or "let go of the past", but in reality, everything is much easier said than done. It is difficult to forgive others that may have wronged us, but it is equally hard to forgive ourselves.

While choosing to forgive yourself is one of the hardest processes you need to go through, the benefits include:

• An understanding that you are human and humans *do* make mistakes.

• An acceptance that you cannot change what you said and/or did in the past, but that you can learn from it.

• A peace inside yourself knowing that you did the best you could under the circumstances.

To start working on forgiving yourself try the following simple, quick exercise. You can use this exercise whenever you realize you may be beating up on yourself.

Exercise:

STEP 1: Think about and answer the question below honestly.

QUESTION: What advice would you give your children or a good friend if they were in the same situation you were in?

For Example:

• Would you tell your child that she should just stay in an unhappy relationship because they are married and obligated to sacrifice?

• Would you tell your child that just because he is unhappy with his marriage *today*, that he will be unhappy forever?

• Would you tell your best friend to "look the other way" and just accept the fact that her husband had an affair?

• Would you tell your child to just accept that her marriage is dull and not meaningful?

• Would you tell your child that his dull/unfulfilling marriage is strictly the fault of his spouse?

Once you forgive yourself, it is time to tackle perhaps the hardest thing you will ever face in your life: forgiving you X.

WHY YOU NEED TO FORGIVE YOUR X

The inability to forgive your X will make you an ongoing victim of your divorce. If you continue to hold on to the transgressions, real or perceived, that have been done to you by your X, that bitterness will block your ability to give and receive love.

Forgiveness is more about focusing on yourself and less about the other person. By choosing to forgive your X, you are no longer a victim of your situation.

> *As Barb made her way across the stage, she reflected on just how far she had come in the last few years. Today, at age 48, she had basically reinvented her life and herself.*
>
> *Barb had married at age 19, raised two children, never had worked outside the home, and at age 44, found her husband having sex in their bed with one of the guests at their silver wedding anniversary party.*
>
> *After her husband admitted that was not the only time he had cheated, Barb left. Although it was difficult to leave the life she had grown accustomed to, and to face the uncertainty of her financial situation, she decided it was better than spending another minute with her husband.*
>
> *In addition to the grief she was experiencing over the loss of her marriage, she was angry, resentful and bitter. Angry at him for what he had done, angry at the women he had slept with, and angry at herself for trusting him. She resented that her life was not turning out the way she had planned, and was bitter that she was broke, and living in a crappy little apartment instead of her nice four-bedroom home. She was blinded by anger, blame and bitterness.*
>
> *Barb's wake-up call came when she was fired from the receptionist job she had recently landed at her dentist's office. She was told that her poor attitude was not in line with the type of employee they needed to greet their patients.*
>
> *Barb realized that the anger she was holding onto about her divorce and the end of her marriage was really affecting her life and that she needed to find a way to let go, forgive the situation and move on.*

That was easier said than done, but she knew that the only person all that anger and bitterness was hurting was her, so she started by working on herself. She found a new entry-level job at a hotel, fixed up her apartment, and started taking night courses at the local community college.

Barb's 'ah-ha' moment came once she understood that forgiveness does not mean that you excuse the other person's behavior and that it is more about allowing yourself to move on. Today, Barb stood on the stage of that community college and received her associate degree in hotel management.

Finding Forgiveness Isn't Always Easy

Part of completing your divorce detox is forgiving your X.

You may be saying, "I can *never, ever* forgive him!"

That may be the case; however, you should rethink that.

The only way you can move past the hate and condemnation you may feel for your X, and move on to loving and growing as a person after your midlife divorce is to forgive him.

After a divorce, and the many years you invested in your marriage and in your X, it's human nature to put some emphasis on it.

As discussed earlier, emotional responses are normal and grieving is a necessary in the divorce recovery process, but remaining stuck in that state is the danger.

Remember, emotional wounds will only begin to heal when, after a time of grieving, you move on with your life. In order to live a full and complete life, you must learn how to forgive your X, so you do not carry the pain, bitterness and disappointment with you into your future.

Anger seems justified in a lot of circumstances. However, forgiveness is a major part of the healing process that can result in a tremendous restoration.

If your divorce was amicable, you may think there is no need to forgive your X, but most likely you are holding on to some blame or resentment and haven't yet forgiven your X.

Hanging on to pain, bitterness and disappointment from the past is a heavy burden. It affects your moods, attitudes, relationships, job and all aspects of your life. Negativity eats away at your self-esteem and destroys any possibility of a life free from pain.

What is forgiveness?

Remember ... Forgiveness isn't about saying that whatever happened during your marriage and during your divorce is irrelevant. Nor does it mean you are condoning inexcusable behavior. It is about you and how forgiving allows you to move on.

Forgiveness releases you from the burden of carrying the pain any longer. By choosing to forgive, you stop thinking about the past and control your future.

Ask yourself these questions to determine if you are on the path to forgiving your X:

• Are you constantly dwelling on specific events from your marriage that have caused you pain?

• Have friends and family started avoiding you because you only talk about your X and how he has done you wrong?

• Does revenge seep into your thoughts?

• Are you still obsessed with how things 'could have been' if it weren't for the divorce?

• Do you think more about your X than you do yourself?

If you answered **YES** to one or more of these questions, then you need to work on forgiving your X. However, before getting into how to begin to forgive your X, the issue of infidelity has to be addressed.

There is no getting around it, infidelity is extremely painful, and unfortunately, as we learned, is a factor in many divorces. While life comes with different experiences and challenges, the emotional impact of infidelity can be staggering, and therefore extremely difficult to deal with, and almost impossible to forgive.

Like an unexpected punch in the stomach, infidelity often hits hard and fast, usually coming out of the blue. Even if you have been harboring suspicions of infidelity for months, the truth — the hard cold reality — never fails to pack a punch. In addition, the emotions that surround infidelity are nothing like you've experienced before.

With no prior experience in dealing with infidelity, it can be difficult to understand and deal with it. Emotions are often paralyzing. While there have been a number of theories and advice on dealing with infidelity, emotions are far too complex to deal with and often undermine your confidence and beliefs.

Acceptance is an important first step, so you can give yourself a break and cut some slack on some of your self-imposed and often unrealistic expectations on how you 'should' feel and react. Understand that all emotions that surround infidelity are valid.

Here are the most common emotions associated with infidelity:

- Great depths of bitterness, anger, resentment and betrayal.
- Sense of loss, great sadness, loneliness and self-doubt.
- Confusing emotions for your X such as tenderness, pity, and love.

Get in tune with each emotion and don't be scared to feel them. It is normal for certain emotions to be conflicting when coming to grips with infidelity.

• • •

Remembering the Love is a Step toward Forgiving Your X

Whether infidelity was a factor in your divorce or not, part of healing and eventually forgiving your X is creating something good out of the bad. To help yourself come to that point, you need to remember the love, and look past the pain, disappointment and hurt your X may have inflicted.

If you have shared several decades of marriage, there are surely some happy memories. Take some time out and try the following exercise to help you remember some of the better times. For this exercise try to remember only some of the good times — think about where you were, what you were doing, how you and your X were acting. Remembering the love and some of the better times will remind you that the man you once married is not really a monster who has ruthlessly broken your heart, that he is human, just like you, and has his own set of good and bad attributes which is a good start toward forgiveness.

Exercise:

STEP 1: Reflect on the happier times.

This is not to rub salt in a wound, but to help you to move toward forgiving your X.

STEP 2: As you remember, try not to re-write history to either make it all good or all bad — both extremes are not healthy or accurate.

No matter how you feel about your marriage and your divorce, you will not be able to deny the fact that your X was a huge part of your past life. This exercise will remind you that not all memories of your past or your X are bad ones.

• • •

4 Ways to Help You Forgive Your X

1. Uncover your anger.

You need to accept that you are hurt, angry at and frustrated with your X. Even though you may have every right to be angry, in order to have the courage to truly forgive your X, you are choosing to let it go.

2. Decide you want to forgive him.

You don't have to wait for your X to own up or realize his mistakes in order for you to forgive him. The virtue of forgiveness is something within you that you can freely give any time you are ready.

3. Think of your X in a new way.

Once you are starting to open up to the idea of forgiveness, you will come to realize that your X may also be angry and hurting. If you just thought "good," you have a bit more work to be done on forgiving your X.

4. Discovering new things about yourself and the rest of the world.

Forgiveness will help you find more meaning in your life. Forgiving your X will enable you to be more open to meeting new and interesting people without looking at them as if they are your X.

WHY IS IT SO IMPORTANT TO FORGIVE YOUR X?

Forgiveness releases you from the burden of carrying the pain any longer.

In order to let go of the pain of your divorce, you have to be aware of the feeling, acknowledge it, and accept, and allow it to go.

Below is a simple pain-releasing exercise, and because our *real problem* is **not** our painful feelings but our *reaction* to them, this exercise will help you let go of the painful reactions. Our reactions can limit our ability to forgive.

Exercise:

STEP 1: Sit somewhere quiet, and think about your X.

STEP 2: What is the first feeling you feel?

STEP 3: Become aware of the feeling. What is it? Use *one* word to describe it.

STEP 4: Acknowledge the feeling, thank it for showing up.

STEP 5: Accept it and imagine yourself writing the feeling on a slip of paper.

STEP 6: Imagine taking that slip of paper and putting it in a bottle.

STEP 7: Now imagine throwing that bottle into the ocean — watch it drift away.

Letting go of painful feelings will enable you to open up room in your head and your heart for forgiveness.

WHAT WILL FORGIVENESS LOOK LIKE?

You will know that have truly forgiven yourself and your X if the memory of your marriage or your divorce no longer has the power to make you feel bad. You will also notice that the memories no longer resurface as often, and when they do, they do not weigh you down with bitterness and sadness.

If you are having trouble with forgiving yourself or your X, remember that working with a therapist or life coach may be what you need to give you the extra tools and encouragement to forgive and move on to live a happy and full second chapter of your life.

!! Forgiveness isn't about saying that whatever happened during your marriage and during your divorce is irrelevant. Nor does it mean you are condoning inexcusable behavior. It is about you and how forgiving allows you to move on.

ENVIRONMENTAL DETOX

In addition to the emotional detoxing after your divorce, there is also a need to do some environmental detoxing. Changing what is around you may help you feel better and move on, especially in situations where you are still in the same house or apartment that you shared with your X. Even if you have moved, you most likely kept a lot of the items that were in your old place, so doing some of the things suggested below will still work for you.

These seemingly simple steps are a great way to reassert your own sense of self. If you are looking forward to redefining yourself and your life after your midlife divorce, why not start with where you live?

Rearrange your home furniture.
If you can't afford the expense of replacing furniture pieces, the simple act of rearranging your existing furniture will give your living

space a new look and feel. Try putting some of the furniture you used to have in your living room in your bedroom — just because it was originally purchased for a certain room doesn't mean that now it can't be used elsewhere.

Clear away things that you don't like.

Get rid of any items that no longer bring you a sense of pleasure. Get rid of pictures or decorative items that you never really liked or that remind you too much of your X and/or your marriage. Now is the time to pack up the wedding pictures sitting on the mantel. Remember, it is now *your* space. Decorate it the way you want.

Redecorate your bedroom.

If you can, buy new beddings for your bedroom. If you can't afford to do that, try looking for items such as some throw pillows or pictures that you already own to change the look of your bedroom up a bit. Add something new to the top of your dresser. Also, if you can repaint your bedroom or add new paintings to the wall, do *something* that will make it feel more like a new room. Get creative!

Clean and reduce the clutter.

Any type of visual chaos actually contributes to stress. Your divorce brought enough stress, so take time to eliminate unnecessary clutter. Take comfort in the fact that you no longer have to deal with your X's mess.

!! Changing what is around you will help you feel better and allow you to move on

Now that we've learned a little bit about grieving your divorce, letting go, and divorce detoxing, it is time to move forward with your divorce recovery and look at your new life and the new you and new possibilities!

CHAPTER X:
THE NEW YOU

"Change gives one the opportunity for re-invention."

After completing your divorce detox, it is now the time to start creating the new you, and once you start, you may just realize that your divorce may just be the best thing that ever happened to you.

This chapter is chock-full of exercises and strategies to rebuild your confidence, identify your life's purpose, as well as tips on how improving your attitude can impact how you live the next chapter of your 'happily ever after.'

REBUILDING YOUR CONFIDENCE

What does confidence look like?

Confidence is knowing you will achieve your goals and meet most of the challenges in life because you are a capable, intelligent, independent woman.

Unfortunately, it is quite normal for women to deal with insecurities during and after a divorce.

So, what does confidence look like?

Below are some characteristics of confidence in women:

• Self-Confident Women Trust Themselves

Confidence is something you possess. Self-confident women trust their decisions, choices, instincts and the knowledge they have based on the experiences they've had in their life.

• Self-Confident Women Are Not Always Right

Although these women have conviction in their abilities and their decision-making, they also know when to take advice and when it's necessary to change course. These women take the time to see things from other people's perspective because they know the importance of having a balanced point of view.

• Self-Confident Women Accept That They Have The Right To Be Happy In Life

A self-confident woman will always go after what she wants, regardless of any obstacles that come up. This is because these women know deep in their heart that they have the right, just like everyone else in the world, to fight for their happiness and to follow whichever path they believe will lead to it.

• Self-Confident Women Learn From Their Mistakes

Making mistakes is just part of life. A self-confident woman will deal with her mistakes, but not dwell on her shortcomings or how things could have been done differently. A confident woman keeps her focus on the future and uses her life experiences as learning tools so she doesn't make the same mistake again.

• Self-Confident Women Don't Compare Themselves With Others

Women have the bad habit of comparing themselves with other women or to the women in magazines or in the movies. This is a waste of valuable energy and is something that self-confident women do *not* do. Confident women realize that there will always be people who are better looking than they are, have more money than do, and are more successful. These women acknowledge and own their own strengths, as well as their weaknesses and they understand that other people have both as well. Confident women do not waste time wishing they were someone else, instead they keep their focus their strengths and where they want to be in life.

!! Confidence is a belief that you will achieve your goals and meet most of the challenges in life because you are a capable, intelligent, independent woman.

BUILDING (OR BUILDING BACK) YOUR SELF-CONFIDENCE

Below is a short exercise to help with regaining some of the confidence you may have lost due to your midlife divorce. It is a simple exercise that you can complete quickly, but that will have a great impact on your confidence and self-esteem.

Exercise:

STEP 1: Get out a paper and pen or open a blank document on your computer.

STEP 2: Looking back on your whole life, make lists of the following:

• List 3 happy memories or good times no matter how short or fleeting.

Example: Your first kiss.

• List 3 things you have won and/or lucky breaks you may have experienced.

Example: Having an interview for a job with someone who shares your love of mystery novels.

• List 3 personal achievements and successes, no matter how small.

For example: Learning to tie your shoe.

• List 5 things you are good at doing.

Note: These do not have to be major things — if you are great at putting on eye makeup then that makes the list.

• List 1 physical attribute you like about your body.

For example: Nice eyes or pretty shoulders or shiny hair.

STEP 3: Read your list every morning for at least a week.

If you take the time to remind yourself of your positive attributes daily, you will see your self-confidence start growing strong after your midlife divorce.

• • •

Assertive You vs. Aggressive You

You may already know this, but the most sought after self-help books are those on how to be confident and assertive. This is because to achieve goals in life, these are the two most important character traits. This is especially true for women who are redefining themselves after a divorce.

Thankfully, if you weren't born with confidence and the ability to be assertive, you can learn them. It is never too late in life to learn, but first you need to learn the difference between being assertive and aggressive.

As you work on your confidence, you will need to assert yourself, as they go hand-in-hand. The thing to remember is that people generally respond better to an assertive person rather than an aggressive person.

Aggressive people are bullies who approach problems with harsh criticism. They would say someone is doing a project "all wrong," for example.

An **assertive** person, on the other hand, approaches the same situation with concerns and ideas to improve the project. "I've had luck in the past doing this. Have you considered trying it this way?" for example.

Your goal should be to approach people with positive attitudes and solutions to problems. If you respect others and treat them as you want to be treated, you'll have the same courtesy returned to you.

To be ASSERTIVE and *not aggressive* try implementing the following:

• **Become informed.**

One of the best methods of being assertive and confident is to know your subject matter. No matter what the situation is, the more you know, the more confident you'll be.

For example: Keep up with current events and read books you enjoy.

• **Speak up.**

Speak with confidence even if you don't feel confident. Practice speaking this way. The more you practice the more it will become second nature.

NOTE: Speaking loudly does *not* equal confidence. If, on the other hand, you are naturally a soft-speaker, increase your tone and volume — it will make you appear and feel more confident.

• **Model your behavior after people you admire.**

Chances are the people you admire have the assertiveness and confidence you're looking for in your own life.

• Observe how they do things.

• Pay attention to what they say and how they say it.

• Watch their body language.

THE NEW YOU BEGINS WITH ACCEPTANCE

Your divorce has given you the opportunity to redefine who you are and who you want to be. In order to do this, you need confidence. Right now, choose to let go of any negative feelings you may have and instead embrace the real you — mistakes and all!

Remember, it's your mistakes, your imperfections, and your experiences that make you the perfectly unique (and confident) woman you are today.

Below are a few additional tips on rebuilding your confidence:

TIP #1: Act confident.
'Fake it, 'til you make it.' Eventually, you will feel as confident as you act.

TIP #2: Accept compliments.
Once your confidence has taken a major blow, like a divorce, it is hard to accept and believe compliments, but you need to start. It is important never to contradict the compliment, instead simply say "thank you."

TIP #3: Walk around with your head held high.
Just the act of standing up straight and holding your chin up will boost your confidence.

TIP #4: Smile.
Learn to smile more often even when you aren't in the smiling mood. Smiling at others, even strangers, will make you seem more approachable, and it is also nice when you get a smile back in return.

YOU ARE BEAUTIFUL!

Before you read any further, remember you are already beautiful, both on the inside and out. However, you have just lived through one of the most stressful things you will ever face in your life, your divorce, and most likely your self-care has taken a backseat to divorce discussions, lawyer appointments, and a million other things.

In order to feel confident and ready to face your new life, it is time to spend some time on yourself. Plus, looking good on the outside will help build up or build back your self-esteem and self-confidence. Also, you are entitled to a little pampering!

Hair Care
Take a trip to the hair salon. Try a new hairstyle. Cut it off, change the color, get bangs or anything that suits your fancy as long as you do

something with your hair. The more extreme, the more liberated you will feel. Nothing says "new you" like a new do!

Check the Closet

Give away anything that is a size small or a size too big for your body. Also get rid of clothes you never wear and clothes that are more suited for women 10 years younger than you or 20 years older. If you have any clothes that invite a lot of weird stares from people when you are wearing them, put them in the give-away pile. In order to feel confident you have to look confident.

Implement a Self-Care Regimen

Women tend to let self-care take a backseat to the other priorities in their life. Now is the perfect opportunity to stop doing that. Decide today that self-care is a top priority. It is just like they say on an airplane ... put your mask on before helping others with theirs. In order for you to be the best you can be, you need to make self-care a top priority.

It is important to know that when you take care of yourself, you make your whole life better. Properly caring for yourself gives you the passion and energy to live life to its fullest with plenty left over to devote to those you love.

It is critical to take this seriously and schedule time every day for self-care. This includes hectic days and especially on stressful days:

Self-Care Ideas:

• Exercise — buy an inexpensive exercise DVD, take a walk, try yoga
• Eat right
• Get enough sleep — turn off the computer, shut the book and get some sleep
• Meditate and say affirmations — good for the mind and the body
• Have some "down time" to read a book or a magazine
• Take time in the morning to really enjoy your coffee or tea
• Get your nails done or do them yourself

• Get a massage
• Take a long, hot bath

It is important to take care of yourself so you can be the best you can be. Remember, when you take a break to do something just for yourself, you'll come back stronger than before with more focus and energy. You'll have enough strength and fortitude to handle whatever life throws your way. Today, plan to spend more time on you!

!! *Remember, you are already beautiful, both on the inside and out.*

NEW YOU, MAYBE NEW CAREER

First we will address careers if you did not have a career outside of your home during your marriage. If that is the case, then you may be collecting child support (if your children are still minors) and possibly some alimony. As you may have already figured out, you cannot live on those things alone.

So, how exactly does one start a career, especially at midlife?

By putting one foot in front of the other, is how. It is never too late to start a career. View this as an opportunity to do something not only for your financial health, but for your emotional health as well.

Before you jump right into searching for a new career, there are a lot of things to consider, such as, the amount of time you want to spend working, what kind of job do you want, and realistically what are you qualified to do.

If you haven't worked outside of the home in a while, you may need to be realistic on the type of job you will be able to get, even if you have a college degree. You may want to consider brushing up some skills to be more marketable when applying for a job. The internet is a great place to take low cost training and courses from the comfort of your own home. Instead of spending nights surfing the internet for information on divorce spend it learning a new skill.

To start you on your way to finding a new career:

Update Your Resume
List all your work experiences you can think of that are transferable.

For example, if you were president of the PTA, then you have leadership skills.

Look the part.
When you are planning to get a job, dress and act as if you already have one. Remember, appearance matters all the time. You must have at least one good outfit that is suited for job hunting.

Don't Always Go the Traditional Route
Nowadays, there are many more opportunities for you to work from home than there had been in years past. Check out the opportunities on the internet; however, be careful as there are a lot of scams that target women who want to work from home. Look for legitimate opportunities that pay you and not the other way around. If a company is looking for money from you in order to give you a job, think twice. Maybe three times!

See This as a Second Chance
If you are able to financially do this, now is the time to decide on a career that you want or have always wanted to have but didn't pursue during your younger years. Go back to college (maybe junior college), take a course at the local technical school, start your own business.

• • •

If you already had a career outside the home while you were married, you may still want to look at a career change. A lot of women who have gone through a midlife divorce decide that it is time for a complete make-over of their lives and that includes their career.

As we already learned, women at midlife use this time to reflect and assess where they are in life and where they want to be. This is a perfect time to rethink a career and make a change.

The key to a successful career change at midlife, and especially after a midlife divorce, is planning. Creating a workable plan and setting goals will get you to the career of your dreams.

There are a lot of good books and programs for midlife career changes, and working with a life coach can also ensure that you get on and stay on track. Remember, you have plenty of time left in the working world, so why not do something you love. You are in control of your life now, so get motivated and get going.

   !! The key to a successful career change at midlife, and especially after a midlife divorce, is planning.

DIGGING A LITTLE DEEPER: FINDING YOUR LIFE PURPOSE

Some might not agree that anyone has a "life purpose." Instead, they think that they are better suited to doing tasks A, B and C, rather than tasks X, Y, and Z. So if this is the way you perceive things, think "doing what you like," as you read "life purpose."

If you want to dig even deeper than just looking at a new career and if your divorce has you questioning why you're here, you may want to spend some time discovering your purpose in life. After all, you have a unique set of passions and talents that no one else in the world has! Discovering your purpose in life lets you use your unique assortment of feelings and abilities to bring you greater self-fulfillment.

When you're doing what you feel like you were born to do, you can create a life you enjoy, and it is never too late to start.

Knowing your purpose will give more meaning to you. Challenges will be easier to overcome because you will be working toward achieving goals that are in line with your true purpose.

Below is an exercise for finding your life purpose. It enables you to tune in to your inner self and figure out what makes you tick.

When is the perfect time to find your purpose? Right now, right after that divorce, as you are creating that new you. You'll find you will be changing for the better.

Again, this exercise may seem a bit 'woo-woo' or 'out there', but try it, it just might work for you.

For this exercise, an open mind is optional, but helpful, although this can work for you even if you don't believe it will work, it just will take a little longer.

To do this exercise you need about a full hour of uninterrupted time, have peace and quiet, a piece of paper and pen or your computer with a blank document pulled up.

During this exercise, try to empty your mind as much as possible. The clearer your mind is, the quicker and easier the process will be.

Exercise:

STEP 1: Focus on your intention. Write at the top of your paper: "This is my life purpose." This simple act sets your intention in your mind for the next hour.

STEP 2: Begin listing your thoughts — even doubts — about this process. As you clear your mind and focus on this process, write whatever comes to mind, no matter what it is. If you think to yourself, "This isn't going to work," then you would write, "This isn't going to work."

STEP 3: Answer these questions and just keep writing. Write down anything that comes into your mind for each question, and keep writing and answering until you feel like you may have uncovered your purpose.

- What are your talents and abilities?
- Which talents would you like to develop further? Why?
- What are your passions?
- Do you get joy from helping others? Who?
- Have you ever wanted to be a philanthropist?

- What activities do you enjoy?
- What have you always wanted to do, but you haven't done it yet?
- Who do you most enjoy being around? Adults? Children? Why?
- Do you love animals?
- Do you like to travel?
- Do you want more excitement in your life?
- What are your favorite books? Why?
- How do you feel about your relationships?
- Do you take an interest in politics or world matters?
- What is the most important priority in your life? Family? Work? Money? Fame? Something else?

NOTE: It is common that answers will repeat themselves. A lot of unrelated nonsense is also likely to come out. Our brains can be a little cluttered, and this exercise will expose that. Don't let anything you write distract you from your intentions; odd things quite frequently end up on the paper.

How will you recognize your purpose?

The idea will resonate with you completely, and there won't be any doubt. Just continue writing whatever comes into your mind until you reach that point. There will be several answers along the path that feel pretty good to you, but remember, you're looking for The One. When you see the ones that are good, but not 'it,' this means you're close, but not quite on target yet. You're looking for that one idea that feels irresistible to you.

In this exercise, it's common for your life purpose to reveal itself in less than 100 ideas, but it can take as many as 400. Keep writing.

How Can I Apply My Life Purpose to Benefit Me?

Now that you've discovered your purpose, you can now always try to honor it. When you are making a decision, always ask yourself, "Is this in alignment with my ultimate purpose?"

A life lived like this, with direction and intentionality, is a life you can truly enjoy. Knowing the core reason you're here is one of the greatest gifts you could ever give yourself.

MOTIVATION TO CREATE YOUR NEW NORMAL

Once the divorce papers are signed and some time passes, you will understand and accept that the 'normal' world of your marriage is over. This may cause you to start questioning what your new normal is.

While it's true that the divorce is the end to your marriage, it is also a chance for new beginnings and better choices. Yes, the relationship may be over with your X, but it is not over with your family, friends and children.

<u>Make more time for new beginnings.</u>
In the past, you most likely had ways of doing things and family traditions. This may have included always going for pizza on Friday nights or Sunday family dinner at your home or Thanksgiving dinner at Uncle Bob's and New Year's Eve at Jack and Jill's house.

After your divorce, things will be different. Different doesn't equal bad. In fact, in this case different equals your motivation to determine how you want tao live your life. Just because you have always done this or that in the past, does not mean that this or that still needs to happen now.

<u>Be open to making new routines and new traditions.</u>
This is the perfect time to experiment and pursue what you really want out of life. It is the motivation to become the woman you want to be. What kind of a person you want to be now?

Once you've answered that question, you have a better idea about what direction to take and what you need to do to take full charge of your destiny. You have full control of your life now. Your midlife divorce may have just been the motivation you needed to live the life you want and to be the woman you want — get motivated!

The following exercise can help you to identify your motivators. Being able to figure out what motivates you will be a real benefit to you not only during your divorce recovery, but to give you a boost, if necessary, to reach a goal.

Exercise:

STEP 1: Think about the most difficult situation you've ever experienced.
NOTE: This may or may not be the decision to divorce.

STEP 2: Answer the following questions.
• What did you think about the situation?
• How did you feel about it?
• How did you arrive at how you were going to handle and resolve the situation?
• What was important to you at the time?
For example, was it how you felt, what you thought others would think, what you believed was 'the right thing to do' or something else?
• Ultimately, what did you do to resolve the situation? Or did you let someone else solve it for you because of your inactivity?

STEP 3: Think about 2 or 3 of your biggest achievements.
Example: Graduating from college or getting your first apartment.

STEP 4: Picking one of the achievements, answer the following questions.
NOTE: This process will help you to identify your own motivations.
• What did you do to achieve your success?
• How did you meet your goals?
• What did you think about during the process?
• What motivated you?
For example, looking out for your future, wanting to make more money, hoping to make your parents proud, or something else?

• Did you visualize what your life would be like once you had achieved your goal?

• How much did you really want to achieve it?

STEP 5: Re-read all your answers from Step 1-4.

STEP 6: After reflecting on the above questions, your mind will be more open to identifying what's important to you. Answer the below questions.

• What have you discovered that motivates you?

• Are you surprised at what you've found?

• How do you feel about these concepts?

It is important to remember that what motivates you may not motivate someone else. The purpose of this exercise is to find out what motivates you!

Even though what motivates you may vary depending on the situation, you will most likely still find that you are inspired by the same one or two motivations consistently throughout your life, regardless of the situation.

Examples of Motivations may include:

• You want to 'do the right thing.'
• You want to make more money.
• You want to make your future better.
• You want to make your children's futures better.
• You feel the need to prove to yourself that you can achieve something.
• You want to be recognized, noticed and admired.
• You like the idea of stepping up to a challenge in your life.
• Seeking variety in life motivates you to try new things.
• You have the need to prove someone's opinion of you was wrong.
• You want to do something in life that 'really makes a *positive* difference.'
• You enjoy the sheer entertainment value of doing something.

• You strive to overcome a difficult childhood and emerge victorious.

• When you are working on something you're passionate about it propels you toward your goals.

• You don't want to disappoint your parents or you strive to make them proud of you (this one never really goes away).

• Discovering and validating who you really are as an individual is important to you.

• Writing down your goals and making an action plan spurs you on to accomplishment.

• You like to see your list of achievements grow.

Whether you want to improve your life, make more money, or follow your passion, knowing what motivates you can help you as you work toward the life you want to be living.

!! While it's true that the divorce is the end to your marriage, it is also a chance for new beginnings and better choices.

HAVE AN ATTITUDE OF GRATITUDE

You have survived your divorce, but do you realize how much you can improve your outlook on life by simply being grateful? This is what is called an 'attitude of gratitude.' If you cultivate an attitude of gratitude you'll actually bring even more happiness into your life including a fulfilling career, health, and stronger relationships.

An attitude of gratitude is truly a magnet for prosperity and success. As we have learned, much of life is about your attitude and your outlook on things.

It's been said that optimists may be wrong, and pessimists may be right about some things, but optimists enjoy the ride more.

As you work on transforming into the new you after your divorce, also work on transforming your attitude. It can change your entire life. How?

• Change your attitude by showing appreciation a little more often.

• Be thankful for what you do have in your life.

Often we see little to be thankful for because we're always thinking about the things we wish we had or what we have lost. This is especially true after a traumatic life-changer like a midlife divorce.

Even if we live in a comfortable home in a nice neighborhood, have plenty of food on the table, and are healthy, we forget to be grateful. We often take the little things for granted. There are so many joys in your life right now that you're likely overlooking.

For example, by reading this book, you are obviously alive and kicking. Isn't the fact that you are still alive something to be thankful for? After all, someone with incurable cancer would think so.

Ask yourself these questions:
"Did the sun rise today?"
If so, be thankful for the gift of light and warmth.
"Did you have work to do today?"
If so, be thankful for the opportunity to earn a living for you and your family.
"Did you eat a nourishing meal today?"
If so, be thankful for the gift of food.
As we all know, 'things could be worse' which is all the more reason to have an attitude of gratitude!

Your good feelings attract more good back to you. For example, if you desire more money, be thankful for the paycheck you just received, no matter how small it may have been. Truly feeling grateful for it attracts more back to you! On the other hand, if you focus on how small your paycheck is, that's a lack mentality, which attracts more lack back to you.

You can start each day on a good note by giving thanks for the gift of this beautiful day when you wake up in the morning. At night, reflect on all the good things from that day. Try feeling gratitude for a week and see what a difference it can make in your life!

Lots of Gratitude = Positive Attitude

It's a fact; those who are grateful are more uplifting and positive. By having a positive attitude, you'll not only feel better, but you'll also enjoy better health because our body, mind, and spirit are so heavily inter-connected.

As mentioned earlier, by having a positive attitude, you'll be a magnet for positive relationships. You'll attract like-minded people who will not only inspire you, but push you further. After all, like attracts like, which is all the more reason to be positive.

Spend a few moments showing your appreciation to your loved ones, colleagues, or any random strangers you meet — it will change your life!

!! *An attitude of gratitude is truly a magnet for prosperity and success.*

Now, with your improved confidence, a new purpose and a new attitude, it is time to move on to the final chapter of this guide which will go over the other D-Word.

CHAPTER XI:
SEE YOU AT 8!

"Let's just call it meeting new people."

As we already know, your midlife divorce has opened up a lot of opportunities for you: self-reflection and reinvention, a new way to live, possibly a new career and just maybe it is time to finally explore the D-word. Not divorce, the other D-word ... Dating!

If your divorce is fresh you may be saying, "No thank you. I've been there, done that."

However, you may find that once some time has passed, and you have taken the necessary time to work on your own personal development, you may decide you would like a new someone to share your life with or you would like to date for the sake of dating — entertainment, companionship, possibly sex. Since you were married for a long time, it has been a while since your last date. Try to remember, dating can be fun!

When you feel you are emotionally ready or if a wonderful person happens to come into your life that you would like to get to know better, this chapter will give you some advice and tips, as well as red-flags you should watch out for when you decide to get back into the dating game. There is also a valuable exercise which will help you to make sure that if you are looking for a 'special someone' or just trying to figure out if there should be a second date, that he has the qualities you want in order to have a fulfilling relationship.

But as with every important decision, trust your instincts. Talk is cheap; gut feelings are not.

GETTING BACK IN THE DATING GAME

Are you ready? Because as you know, midlife divorce is traumatic and everyone's divorce recovery timetable is different, it is important that you really know you are ready before you venture out into the great dating scene. It is equally important to always keep your mind and heart open to all the possibilities life has to offer.

Below are some areas that you should work on before getting back in the game:

Know Yourself

This is the best gift you can give to yourself. Work on your personal development, and really get to know who you are and how you are really doing emotionally. You may have lost the real you while you were married because your world revolved around your X and raising kids, so your divorce is your opportunity to really bring out or rediscover the real you.

If you start out dating knowing who you really are, what your values are, and where and what you want out of life, you will be more successful meeting people who are in line with the real you, and you will have more fun.

Do Not Settle

This may sound a bit rude, and you should already know this, but you do not have to say yes to every person who asks you out.

If you feel like you have to lower your standards and not be picky due to loneliness or insecurity, then you are *not* ready to date. Spend more time on personal development.

When you are ready, you need to go into the dating world, confident, secure and knowing what type of person you want to date.

Keep Your Expectations Realistic

Go out on a date because you want to again enjoy the dating process and not because you want to get married as soon as possible. Even though you may have had a husband in your life for decades, it doesn't mean that you need to find an immediate replacement.

Enjoy the time you have to be alone, and the ability to focus all your attention on yourself. Enjoy dating, just for dating's sake — companionship and some fun. You don't need to try to turn every date into your next husband.

Divorce Talk

When you are ready to go out on a date, maybe the first few dates are the perfect time to get all of the X (and divorce) talk — yours and his — onto the table so that you understand each other. You certainly don't have to dwell on the negative stuff, but you should know some basic information: # of kids, number of times married, parents living at his or your place, any kids with special needs, any warrants out for his arrest ... you know, things like that.

However, maybe the goal, for *this* date, is to go out, do something, thoroughly enjoy yourselves, and to hell with everything else for a few hours.

This will depend on you (and him), the particular night or the mood.

If It Is a Disaster

If for some reason, your very first date since your midlife divorce is a wreck, don't take it to heart. Those things are bound to happen, especially if you haven't dated in a very long time. The good news is you survived going on a date, even if it was a disaster, so saddle up and get back on the horse. You may find the next one will go a lot smoother — much like everything in life, dating will get easier the more you do it.

Of course this is a subjective thing. What you might think is a disaster, another might consider normal or even a great time. If you're not used to dating, it can be intense, unsettling, even intimidating (not in a physical sense). Particularly that first time out.

!! *When getting back into the dating game after your midlife divorce, remember to know who you really are, what your values are, and where and what you want out of life; never lower your standards due to loneliness; don't look for a replacement husband right away; and most importantly, if a date is a disaster, try, try again.*

A FEW DATING TIPS FOR YOU

TIP #1: Appearance
There are studies saying that attraction is about 75% appearance or image. Let's be honest, you wouldn't be attracted to someone who looks sloppy, dirty, and outdated, right? So, why would he?

TIP #2: Believe
There's no easier way to look attractive than to feel it. It really starts with how you think of yourself and how you feel inside. Stop comparing yourself to younger women or women on TV and in magazines — real life doesn't come with an airbrush, and most men, just like most dogs, like some meat on the bones.

TIP #3: Be Yourself
Never be someone you are not, unless you are playing a part in a movie. Remember, women who are true to themselves and accept who they really are naturally more attractive.

LITTLE RED FLAGS OF POST-DIVORCE DATING

You can actually steer clear from unnecessary issues and heartache when you know which warning signs to look out for when you get back into the dating game. Dating at midlife is a bit different from when you were younger.

The following are some red flags that you can keep an eye out for:

RED FLAG: The X

Being overly involved with the X is a major red flag. To be fair though, you too have an X; however, the red flag will start waving if you realize he spends an inordinate amount of time talking or spending time with his X. This may indicate that he has not moved on, and this is really not a good way to start a new relationship.

RED FLAG: Reeking of Desperation

Desperation is a red flag — both his or yours. Being lonely is not enough of a basis for starting a new relationship. Unless, of course, both of you agree that it *is*.

RED FLAG: Expecting Perfection

While it is understandable that this time around you only want what is best for you, you still need to realize that there isn't one individual that is perfect. Everyone has flaws, including you, and you shouldn't expect a person to change so that they meet some unrealistic criteria that you have established. If you find yourself comparing him to a checklist then that is a red flag — for you, not him. Step back and remember that respect for each other's individuality should always be part of any relationship.

RED FLAG: Too Much of a Good Thing

Obsession and jealousy are traits that are red flags in any relationship, whether it is a new relationship or not. If you find yourself being too clingy or too dependent or too jealous, notice the red flag waving in your face, and it is time to put a little distance into this relationship. This goes the same if he is demonstrating these traits.

!! *Keep your eye out for dating red flags.*

ONLINE DATING

Dating is fun and exciting, but that is true only when you are ready and open for new relationships, and now there are many new ways to find dates. One of the more popular methods is online dating, but like any regular way of dating, online dating also has its pros and cons.

Below are some of the PROS and CONS of online dating:

PROS

• It is a good venue for single people to scan and choose who they would want to date. There are literally thousands of profiles you can actually browse through before starting to send the first "hello" to someone.

• The level of rejection on online dating is different from that of the regular dating. Because it initially takes place on the computer, it is informal. If the initial conversation via email or texting isn't working, it is much easier to end it and not proceed.

• Online dating is a great way for you to actually communicate and get to know each other's interests before meeting. You will get to know the other person and he will get to know who you are inside before the in-person dating happens. If you two do decide to meet, you both will feel more relaxed and comfortable because you already know a little bit about the person already.

• You can filter who you really want to be in contact with.

• You can limit what personal information you reveal.

• It is one way of boosting your ego. When you sign up and put your profile in there, there's a very good chance you will get noticed, and that there are men who will find you interesting.

CONS

• Some profiles on dating sites are just plain fake. There are people who aren't honest about who they really are or what they really look like.

• There can be perverts and creeps trolling these sites, make sure you read the website's policies and stay alert. Never give out too much personal information online, no matter how trusting the other person seems.

• You will miss out on the fun in dating: the going out, meeting and being social. Online dating should be just the first step. A relationship must include face-time, not just webcam-time.

• Friends or family members, and this happens a lot, may not approve of you dating online.

• It can cost you money if you want to broaden your searches. Some sites charge for membership and promise you a better and wider choice. As always, do your research to make sure you aren't paying for services you are not receiving.

• You can actually end up falling for someone who is really married or still in the process of divorce.

• • •

Now that you have a better understanding of the pros and cons of online dating, for your convenience there are some of the more popular online dating websites listed at the back of this book. Since everything on the internet changes, almost daily, keep in mind that these sites are based on information available at the time of writing this book — by the time you check them out, they may either no longer exist, have changed or there may be new ones to add to this list. Use the list as a general guideline, as it was intended.

I have to say kudos to these online dating websites. They simply make dating a lot easier. Of course, you have to remember that dating online is just like any regular dating — it may be for you or may not be and it may work and it may not.

!! *Always put your safety first when dating — online or off.*

A SPECIAL SOMEONE

If finding a 'special someone' that you genuinely want to spend your life with is one of the key ingredients in your recipe for a happy life, then go for it. It is never too late in life to find that 'special someone' who is a lover, companion, trustworthy confidant that you truly want to spend the next chapter of your life with.

Having someone special in our lives is a precious gift. We all appreciate feeling validated and having someone to share our happiness.

Being able to recognize what qualities are important to you when you are looking for love, especially the second time around, will help you choose wisely.

Below are four qualities that are fundamental to successful, loving relationships:

QUALITY: Character

• Are they available, physically and emotionally?
• For a loving relationship, both parties must be available for love. As we have already learned if one of you is already involved with another person or if one of you is still involved with an X, then you're already off to a difficult start.
• Look at how they manage conflicts.
• It's okay to disagree as long as you respect each other's positions. Arguments can even bring you closer together when you both aim for solutions that satisfy both parties rather than seeking to win.
• Trust is basic to any stable relationship. You are worthy of having a relationship that enhances your peace of mind, rather than creating new anxieties.

QUALITY: Background

• How they resolved past issues.

• Regardless of what hardships a person has faced, focus on what they did to overcome adversity and challenges. At your age, everyone you meet, including yourself will come with some 'baggage.'

• Discuss previous relationships.

• People have different comfort levels when it comes to talking about past lovers. Still, it's important to be aware of any patterns and know how to manage them.

• Learn from each other's family history.

• Our family experiences often have a profound influence in shaping our lives and our reactions to new events. For example, knowing how he felt about his divorce might help you understand him better.

• Find common ground on money matters.

• Get a sense of how compatible you are when it comes to making decisions about spending and saving. Many successful people have different perspectives, so you will need to work it out by balancing each other's strengths and weaknesses.

• Know each other's expectations about blending your families before making a commitment.

• Clarify whether you're on the same page.

QUALITY: Personality

• Communicate.

• Constructive communication is the lifeline for any relationship. Communication skills can be improved with practice, but it's helpful to know each other's habits.

• Have fun together.

• After all, you're looking for someone whose company you'll enjoy.

• Share common interests.

• Liking some of the same things will also help you feel more connected.

QUALITY: Chemistry

• Let the sparks fly.
• Physical attraction is one of the greatest joys in life, at any age. There is no age limit on great sex. As long as all the other elements for a healthy relationship are in place, there is nothing wrong with wanting to find someone who makes your heart race and your toes curl in bed.
• Stay healthy.
• If he leads a healthy lifestyle, you may be more likely to preserve that initial attraction. You may even be rewarded with having more years to spend together.
• Take a balanced view of romance.
• It's great to keep romance alive so long as it's free from illusions. As you know from experience, passions will fluctuate over time, but your sense of commitment and affection can keep on growing through the years.
To take a deeper look at the qualities you want in a 'special someone', try the exercise below. It will help you identify the qualities that are important to you when finding that 'special someone.'

Exercise:

Taking the time to understand the qualities that you are looking for and the qualities you bring to a relationship will help you to recognize these qualities when you see them.

STEP 1: List the qualities you want your potential 'special someone' to exhibit?
Such as:

• How does he show me affection?
• How does he make me feel special?
• How does he make me laugh?
• What does he do when I'm sick in bed?
• How does he treat me in front of others when we are in public?
• His most important quality is ...

• The best thing about him is ...

STEP 2: Repeat Step 1, but this time list the qualities **you** will bring to the relationship?

STEP 3: Think about how you will recognize and know if someone has the qualities you listed in Step 1. To do this write down some examples of how he will express the qualities on your list and the associated behavior he will demonstrate.

An example:

How does he treat me in front of others when we are in public?

Qualities: He is *respectful, thoughtful* and *attentive.*

Behavior: He is **respectful to the waitress**, and **he asks me how my day was** and **actively listens** when I tell him.

By completing this exercise you will have a better chance in finding a 'special someone' that will have the qualities that you value when pursuing a loving, caring long-term relationship.

!! If you take the time to care for yourself and learn about your wants and desires you will bring far more to a relationship and be far more successful in finding 'someone special' that has the qualities you need to have a happy, loving, fulfilling long-term relationship.

CONCLUSION

Going through and getting past a midlife divorce may be the most difficult chapter in your life that you've ever encountered. As you know, you are forced to face multiple challenges and changes including the loss of the foundation that had kept you stable during your married years.

Midlife divorce and the divorce recovery process require you to look at just about everything in your life in a new way. As you have learned, you can't just snap your fingers and be fully recovered from your divorce — it is a process, and that takes time.

My hope is that the information, strategies, exercises and ideas in this guide inspire you to see past your midlife divorce and give birth to a new and better you. That you pick up the pieces and start embracing life, including examining and defining yourself, exploring new places, enjoying a rewarding career, meeting new friends, and possibly falling in love again.

My greatest hope is that you do not allow your divorce to define you as a person and dictate your course in life. You have been given a fresh new start, claim it!

The end of your marriage is merely an end to one chapter in your life. It's time you focus on writing a new success story. Whether you make the decision to do it with a new prince charming or as an independent woman, it is possible after your divorce to rewrite your 'happily ever after'.

!! *Make the next chapter in your life count!*

With loving thoughts — *Diane*

POPULAR ONLINE DATING WEBSITES

Match.com
This site tops the list as it is the most comprehensive site when it comes to finding your match. They have a lot of members of more than 20 million, and a variety of search options.

pof.com (Plenty of Fish)
This makes it to the second spot as this is a completely free. There are reportedly millions of people using POF to search for the one every single day. They are also famous for their 'chemistry' test.

eharmony.com
If you want a more scientific approach to finding a good match then eHarmony does just that. They use a model to match individuals based on compatibility. This is especially good for you as this will lessen your burden in finding a match. You just sit there and let them worry about finding the one for you. The website also boasts of the magic they have done on matching up people. According to them, about 542 people who get married in the United States every day are couples that met through their website.

okcupid.com
Like pof.com, okcupid is another free dating website. Members state that they like how easy it was for them to sign up on the website. They are well-known for the quizzes that members take. Aside from instant messages and emails, they also welcome blogs and public forums. They actually do the matching by using user-generated data and the quizzes they have set-up.

zoosk.com
Zoosk is an online dating website that makes use of third-party applications on a number of social networking services. They claim they have more than 50 million single members. Members have the option to subscribe for free or with a fee. However, you will need to pay the fee to fully take advantage of their site. You can also get their services on mobile phones.

CPSIA information can be obtained at www.ICGtesting.com
Printed in the USA
LVOW08s0859040516

486613LV00001B/106/P